CUBA
The Making of a Revolution

Cuba

The Making of a Revolution

BY RAMON EDUARDO RUIZ

THE UNIVERSITY OF MASSACHUSETTS PRESS 1968

Copyright © 1968 by
The University of Massachusetts Press
All rights reserved
Library of Congress Catalog Card
Number 68-19675
Set in Melior and Linotype Primer
by Westcott & Thomson, Inc.
Printed in the United States of America
Designed by Richard Hendel

Para Natalia, Olivia y Maura

Preface

In offering this interpretation of the Cuban Revolution, I am
indebted to scores of writers whose works are acknowledged
in the Bibliography, to many Spanish American intellectuals
who shared their ideas with me, and especially to Mexican
scholars who, in the comfort of their homes, discussed the
Cuban question from their perspective and gave generous
counsel. I thank particularly Eduardo Suárez, former rector of
the Universidad de Nuevo León in Monterrey, Mexico; Salomón
González Almazán, my colleague at the Facultad de Economía of the Universidad de Nuevo León; and my nationalistic students at the Facultad.

Above all, my special appreciation goes to Howard Quint,
who took time from a busy schedule to read the manuscript
carefully and offer countless suggestions for its improvement.
I also thank Howard Wiarda and Warren Dean for their valu-
able criticisms and suggestions. Obviously, I am responsible
for all errors.

Northampton, Massachusetts
January, 1968

Contents

CUBA
The Making of a Revolution

1.

The Cuban Paradox

*These revolutionists are not worms turning,
not children of despair. These revolutions
are born of hope, and their philosophies are
formally optimistic.*

CRANE BRINTON

[I]

Cuba presents Americans with the perplexing paradox of a
relatively rich country which underwent a major social cata-
clysm. Until 1958 the island was simply another Caribbean
republic, the "sugar plantation" of the world; yet that monocultural economy, the target of bitter and persistent criticism,
had produced one of the highest standards of living in the
Western Hemisphere. Judged by the extremes of the North
American "paradise" and the inferno of Haiti, the poorest of
the Caribbean republics, Cuba was a purgatory. But, to the
surprise of the experts, it was Cuba and not its poverty-
burdened neighbors that had a social revolution.

[II]

Although no one can say precisely why a radical upheaval engulfed the island in 1959, Cuba's history contains the key to the probable causes. The shape and course of the Revolution were determined primarily by internal circumstances which were the products of a special society. Foreign events helped to transform the Revolution, but the transformation would have been impossible if the particular historical development of Cuban society had not encouraged it.

Fidel Castro voluntarily embraced the Soviet Union and Communism. The State Department during the Kennedy and Eisenhower administrations was not directly responsible for this realignment of Cuban diplomatic and economic policy. Obviously, one cannot gloss over the historical impact of American foreign policy on Cuban thinking, as Theodore Draper frequently does, but he is essentially correct when he states that Castro turned to the Communist bloc without either having requested or having been refused aid by the United States. But whether or not Castro ever requested American aid is peripheral. Because of the strident anti-Americanism of his revolutionaries, any request by Castro for such aid would have been totally inconsistent.

Cuban leaders could not accept aid from the United States because achieving the radical reforms aspired to in 1959 required the repudiation of a Cuban society that had relied on such support. In the minds of the rebels, indigenous ills had resulted from Cuba's close ties to the United States. Therefore, Castro's integrity as a leader, and that of the Revolution he symbolized, depended on the extent to which he remained free of former commitments to America.

Castro's plans for Cuba's future almost certainly necessitated the nationalization of American sugar properties and the petroleum industry. The resultant clash between the two countries was virtually inevitable, given the predictable

United States attitude toward Cuba's new policies. Washington cannot be absolved of its share of blame for the rupture of relations in 1961, for the Eisenhower administration, with its stress on the role of private foreign investment in Latin America, could hardly have tolerated Castro's attack on American capital.

Nevertheless, it would be a mistake to say that Washington alone was responsible for the conflict between the two countries. International competition between the Russians and the United States for world supremacy proved a decisive factor in the rupture of Cuban-United States relations. Because this global rivalry provided Castro with alternatives denied previous rulers of Cuba, he was able to brush aside American objections to his program by turning instead to the Soviet Union for aid. The East-West rivalry enabled Castro to find a solution to the island's difficulties, but he did not bring with him a new awareness of internal problems, a greater sense of frustration, or solutions other than those proposed by Cuban reformers of the past. Castro relied on old ideas to effect his Revolution, capitalizing on the new international situation to enact socio-economic reforms long envisaged by nationalistic and youthful reformers. With the backing of the Soviet Union, he could pursue his plan to turn the great sugar estates into state-owned farms producing sugar for the markets of the Soviet bloc. Soviet willingness to provide oil made possible Castro's expropriation of American-owned refineries that had kept Cuba supplied with fuel. Meanwhile, the Cuban Communist party offered him an opportunity to consolidate the workers behind his regime.

Although it is true that the ideological shift which occurred when Cuba embraced Marxism-Leninism in 1961 marked an abrupt departure from a neo-capitalistic system and the old reliance on the United States, the Revolution did have roots in national development. There was continuity between the thwarted revolution of 1933 and the upheaval of 1959, and both reflected the mood of the independence struggle of 1895. The new Marxism had roots not only in the Cuban Communist party, the most successful in Spanish America, but in the island's labor movement—which Marxists of varying hues had built in the 1930's and dominated until the late 1940's.

It is anything but certain that Castro was a Communist before 1959. More probably he followed the precedent of other well-known Cubans, such as the Mellas, Roig de Leuchsenring, and Baliños, who turned Communist only after much soul-searching and thought. Further, as the island's pre-1958 history illustrates, Cubans had never emphasized the virtue of political secrecy. If young Castro was a Communist before his victorious entry into Havana, that story was the best-kept secret in a land notorious for rumors and gossip.

Americans were baffled by what transpired after 1959. Since few had taken the time or trouble to study Cuba, contemporary events were generally interpreted with only a superficial knowledge of the island's history and society. Nearly all published studies focused on Cuba's relations with the United States, and primarily on problems that resulted from the island's reliance on an American-dominated sugar industry. Most Americans were totally unaware of the psychological impact of this pattern on Cuban character, thought, and aspirations. Yet political, social, and economic events from 1898 to 1959 had foreseeable consequences. Each generation of the young and hopeful had tasted the bitter fruit of defeat and frustration; all had seen their nationalist dreams thwarted. For instance, the generation that had won independence had to accept limited sovereignty, and that of the twenties lost its revolution in 1934. The youth of the fifties lived in a society of alienated intellectuals and bankrupt politicians, whom Fulgencio Batista had manipulated, and of economic barons who had made their peace with him.

The triumphant Revolution of 1959 represented no sharp break with the past; instead, as Castro has said, it climaxed a long historical struggle, the ultimate success of which had been dreamed of by people who began to fight in the nineteenth century. Nor were the tactics of the Revolution either new or original. From the day in 1953 that Castro and his militants attacked Fort Moncada until the victory of 1959, the revolutionaries copied a pattern of action nearly a hundred years old. The guerrilla warfare adopted in 1956, writes Armando Hart, one of Castro's intimate friends, followed a blueprint that dated back to the nineteenth century, the architects of which were the mulatto warrior Antonio Maceo and the men of 1895 who, inspired and led by José Martí, initiated the final battle for independence. Only national Communism was an innovation, and even that was not entirely alien to Cuban history.

The paradoxical story has another side. The almost total dependence of the Republic of Cuba on the United States had negative as well as positive repercussions. Although the Cubans had been helped economically by America, foreign tutelage had had a deleterious effect on the Cuban mind. It engendered frustration and rage, especially among the young, over the island's inability to travel alone on the road to nationhood. This frustration fed the intense nationalism which underlay the three revolutionary episodes of 1895, 1933, and 1959, and transformed it into a veritable cult of self-pity and resentment.

These sentiments were the product of long domination by the United States. For more than a hundred years of colonial life Cubans had been the stepchildren of a declining Spain which was compelled, on more than one occasion, to reject brash American bids for the island. No sooner had Cuba achieved independence from Spain than it was forced by the United States to accept the Platt Amendment, which severely circumscribed the island's freedom of action. The winning of independence, and later the implementation of the ideal, required a militant nationalism which politicians learned to wield effectively for domestic purposes. Castro was not the first *politico* to exploit fear of imperialism. Nearly every Cuban intellectual had done so, invariably blaming the Wall Street dragon for the island's difficulties. Anti-American tirades were familiar reading. Although they were frequently tongue-in-cheek or simply patriotic propaganda, the youth of Cuba believed them. Castro and his patriots were among the naive who accepted the simplistic diatribes. Ironically, hundreds of these former critics of the United States, who certainly influenced the thinking of their current enemies in Havana, are now in Miami.

Inconsistently, however, no Spanish-American republic displayed a greater interest in American customs and products than Cuba. In less than six decades of independence from Spain, the island had frenetically discarded the vestiges of an Iberian tutelage four centuries old and indiscriminately absorbed American ways. Culturally, economically, and politically, Cuba was the most North American of the former Spanish colonies.

Cuba's historical affinity with English America dated back nearly two centuries. In 1762 the English Royal marines captured Havana, and Cuba began a new era in its history. The island prospered under the British invaders, who introduced new methods of scientific inquiry, the concept of religious toleration, the first Masonic lodges in Latin America, and, perhaps more significant for the future, direct trade with Europe and the British colonies. The island's ties with the Thirteen Colonies, then on the verge of their own independence, survived the American Revolution. At the same time the Cubans established no enduring relationships with the rest of Spanish America.

Nowhere else in Spanish America were fear of and admiration for the United States so intensely juxtaposed. Cubans who were bitterly critical of "American imperialism" copied their northern neighbors in innumerable ways. In the process of imitation, Cuban taste was drastically modified and the local culture became less Spanish, more American and, paradoxically, Cuban.

Affluent Cubans invariably specified, *"Americano, por favor";* only old-line families still preferred products made in France or in Spain. In 1954 the inhabitants of Havana, which had the hallmarks of an American city, purchased more Cadillacs per capita than the natives of any other city in the world; another American product, the Chrysler Imperial, ranked second on the list of preferred automobiles. Although Cubans speak a mongrel tongue which purists refer to as "Spanglish," an American visitor to the island could always find someone who spoke English. Frequently, children of the wealthy were sent away to school in the United States. Cuba's poet laureate, Nicolás Guillén, complained that stories and games for Cuban children were inspired by such American heroes and heroines as Little Orphan Annie and Nick Carter, who preached racial superiority and brute force. Nothing better revealed the imitativeness of the Cubans than their avid devotion to baseball.

Cuban leaders also imitated America politically. Not only was the Constitution of 1901, and to some extent that of 1940, modeled after the American prototype, but the division of Cuba into six provinces reflected the political structure of the United States. Even the famous system of readings in the tobacco factories, which included propaganda favoring independence, developed in imitation of the public readings popular in the United States.

Economically, Cuba profited from its association with the United States, ranking in 1958 as one of the most advanced countries in the Spanish-speaking world. To those Cubans satisfied with the status quo, their country had, in the words of W. W. Rostow, reached the "take-off" stage. According to statistics of the Banco Nacional de Cuba for 1956, per capita income was 336 pesos (the peso was on a par with the dollar)

—the second highest in Latin America. The national sugar industry was a highly mechanized system, operating in conjunction with one of the three highly developed railway networks in Latin America and with up-to-date highways and ports. On a per capita basis, Cuba was the most heavily capitalized of the Hispanic-American countries, and second in gold reserves and foreign trade. Only Mexico, Brazil, and Chile outranked Cuba in the value of industrial production. One of every five Cuban laborers was a skilled worker, while over two-thirds of the population could read and write—a figure surpassed only by the "European" countries of South America. Cuba ranked third in the number of physicians, first in the number of television stations and receiving sets; only North Americans attended movies more frequently than Cubans. For these and other advantages, United States citizens, capital, and skill were at least partly responsible. The island, observed Arthur M. Schlesinger, Jr., was the perfect test for the thesis of the Eisenhower administration that "unhampered private investment was Latin America's road to salvation."

To those who believe that poverty and exploitation are the prime movers of social revolution, the Cuban Revolution is therefore puzzling. The fact is, however, that movements of this sort do not spring from the depths of despair. To paraphrase Leon Trotsky's dictum: If dire poverty bred revolutions, the poor of the world would be in a state of constant rebellion. Social upheavals occur not where people have to grovel daily for a livelihood but, on the contrary, where economic development permits thinking and planning for the future. Cuba had a revolution because it had a measure of economic development. Cuba had, as Schlesinger puts it, "enough wealth about to reveal to all how agreeable wealth might be." The majority of the population was poor, but not so ignorant that it could not visualize a better life for itself if certain structural changes were implemented. The poor in Cuba did not believe that the conditions under which they lived were unalterable, that God had willed the few to live at the expense of the many. Because the poor could think in terms of progress, they believed that with wise leadership and organization they could improve their status.

Yet the question of social revolution rests not merely on the issue of economic development, but more precisely on the degree of social justice. Are the majority of the people, and particularly the emerging middle classes, receiving a just share of the fruits of economic development? Has national progress satisfied "rising expectations?" The facts demonstrate that, in the opinion of many Cubans, economic progress had not brought about a sufficient degree of social justice for all Cubans. Schlesinger concedes that there were "shocking disparities in the distribution of wealth, especially between city and countryside and between white and Negro." Furthermore, statistics do not reveal a growing equality in the distribution of income. Only a fraction of the population enjoyed a monthly per capita income of 540 pesos, while the majority of rural families survived on seven pesos. The rising cost of living, as the table below demonstrates, had sharply reduced real income. Cuba's per capita income was only 336 pesos in 1956 in comparison with Mississippi's $829, the lowest per capita income in the United States. These comparative figures are relevant because the Cubans compared themselves to Americans, not to other Latin Americans.

Year	Per Capita Income at Current Prices	Per Capita Income at 1945 Prices
1945	228	228.0
1951	344	134.7
1952	354	159.5
1953	301	161.8
1954	304	107.1
1955	312	112.4
1956	336	120.9

In these statistics there is an indispensable clue to the character of the Cuban Revolution and the path it subsequently took. Economic progress had encouraged the growth of a sizeable middle sector, which had both profited and suffered from the peculiar nature of economic development. Paradoxically, the middle sector had only a fringe role to play in the island's economic life because a favored coterie of wealthy Cubans and foreigners had a tight grip on the sugar economy, forcing ambitious outsiders to remain on the periphery. Economically, the middle sector was the most frustrated of the groups in Cuba. It was well off, but not sufficiently so to satisfy its appetite for a greater share of the economic and political benefits of Cuban progress.

Denied a full share of the economy, the Cuban middle sector turned to political activity. From 1940 to 1952 politicians of this sector had more or less controlled the political apparatus. The Auténticos, the party of Ramón Grau San Martín and Carlos Prío Socarrás, won the national elections of 1944 and 1948, and individual members of the middle sector held political posts at the local, state, and national levels from the twenties. Despite the tardy collaboration of Batista and his sergeants, the frustrated revolution of 1933 was essentially the contribution of the middle sector.

Unfortunately for Cuba, the middle-sector politician failed to offer able class or national leadership. Instead, more frequently than not, he coveted public office for personal profit, thereby making both the middle sector and the nation suffer. Ultimately, the politicians formed a distinct and separate class, which was castigated for its disregard of the public good, and by 1958 had little prestige among the people of Cuba.

The Cuban experience casts doubts on the validity of the theory popular among some political scientists who envisage the salvation of Latin America in terms of middle-sector rule. For in Cuba, where the middle sector exercised political power, it totally discredited itself and, in the eyes of lower-class Cubans, the system of representative government. The lower classes saw themselves as no better off under the middle-sector politicians than they had been under the former insurgents and sugar barons of the era from independence to 1940.

One explanation for the failure of middle-sector government was its lack of cohesiveness. Theodore Draper errs when he ascribes a "middle-class way of life" to "middle class" Cuban families. Furthermore, contrary to his claim, Cuba had not "already" undergone "its bourgeois revolution." That nebulous stratum between the upper and lower echelons of Cuban society was made up not of one but of several sectors, none of which, either separately or as a whole, had a consciousness of class. Because each part of the middle sector had its own needs, no consensus or unanimity of opinion united the various sectors. Suffering along with other segments of the population from the hard times and political morass of the fifties, the middle sectors were unanimous only in their aspiration to join hands with the more affluent. The middle sectors had been compelled to assume the role of a permanent middle class, which they were unwilling to do.

But the fact that middle-sector unrest existed does not prove that the Revolution was middle class. Castro's rambling speech at the Moncada trial, a potpourri of middle-class panaceas, quasi-Marxist remedies, and paternalistic attitudes, eventually received public approval from the middle sectors, but for varied and conflicting reasons. Each of the middle sectors thought it perceived its own special indictment of Cuban ills in Castro's analysis of Cuba's problems. Later, the various sectors were to disagree vociferously, with Castro and among themselves, over what Castro had promised and about what Cuba needed in the way of reforms. Therefore, to allege, as Draper does, that the Revolution was monolithically "middle class" and that Castro betrayed it when he adopted non-middle-class goals, is to ignore the complexity of the truth. The Revolution had neither a self-conscious middle class at its helm nor well-defined middle-class objectives. Instead, it had the backing and leadership of middle sectors which could not agree on a common program. Ultimately, Castro and his coterie of youthful malcontents, the most frustrated of the middle sectors, imposed their program on the others, and the Communists joined the Fidelistas.

The Revolution had few leaders outside of those from the nebulous and divided middle sectors, the most notorious example being Castro himself, the son of a planter. Labor remained aloof from the Revolution; only the upheaval of 1933 had drawn the worker into its vortex. In the general strike of that year, the worker had advanced beyond the protest advocated by his leaders; labor radicals had even organized "rural soviets" in the sugar mills. In 1933, however, jobless and hungry men had been driven to extreme measures, but no such motivation existed in 1958. The worker was not living in conditions of intolerable poverty. The urban worker, especially, remained more or less neutral in the conflict between Batista and his enemies. Not once did organized labor heed Castro's call for a general strike. In the earlier struggle against Gerardo Machado, the Communists had fomented work-stoppages, but they opposed Castro until the summer of 1958. Blas Roca, one of the Communist stalwarts, called Castro and his circle "petty bourgeoisie."

Nor did peasants furnish the leadership or provide the program of the Revolution. Castro's Revolution was not a peasant revolution, for Cuban peasants formed only a tiny minority of the rural workers who labored on the tobacco farms or sugar plantations—which were more like factories than farms. To cite Draper, the few peasants or *guajiros* in the Sierra Maestra "were utterly alien to" Castro and his cohorts. That *guajiros* later supplied the rebels with food, as Ernesto Guevara claimed, is true; but since Castro's small band never numbered more than 300 guerrillas, only a fraction of the rural population participated directly in the armed conflict. Not until the guerrillas had virtually triumphed, late in 1958, did the people of the countryside join the vocal supporters of the Revolution. Castro's agrarian promises ultimately awakened a rural discontent which, although it had remained dormant throughout most of the period of anti-Batista protest, was easily kindled and provided Castro with the backing he later sorely needed.

The Revolution moved with astonishing speed. One reason for this can be found in the absence of insuperable barriers in its path. Cuban society was weak. Split by economic, social, and ethnic divisions, it was a dependent society, the child of American tutelage and of Spanish rule. As noted, no homogenous middle class or national bourgeoisie existed, while the welfare of both the middle sectors and the sugar barons depended on the United States. Neither group had a clearly defined or class interest to defend; both were international in character, more reliant on foreign interests than on local factors. Politically, Cuba had reached the end of an era; parties and politicians were bankrupt, and therefore the structure of society simply crumbled. The guerrilla phase of the Revolution lasted a short two years, and fighting was sporadic and limited in territorial scope. Castro's militants alone did not vanquish Batista; the *caudillo* fell because he lost the support of the politically aware segments of the population. The government contributed to its own defeat. Without the inherent weakness of Cuban society and Batista's own mistakes, Castro's band could not have triumphed.

Similarly, the absence of ideology in the Fidelista camp characterized the prerevolutionary picture, for Cuba lacked a concise national ideology or set of universal beliefs. Of the political groupings, the Communists alone provided ideological and political unity. They had successfully organized and controlled union labor in the thirties and forties and offered Castro the discipline, organization, and ideology he needed to rally the workers behind him. Confronted with the need for political allies and sharing a similar analysis of Cuban history and ills, Castro turned to them.

Further, Cuba suffered from a state of moral bankruptcy. The Cuban people had lost faith in themselves and in their leaders. "It is difficult," the Cuban scholar Luis Aguilar perceptively recognized, "to meet a more skeptical and distrustful people than ours." Nor had economic stagnation or political dishonesty alone produced this moral turpitude; the crisis went deeper. To Aguilar it stemmed from a profound debasement of national ideals which should have sustained the politician as well as the worker, the landlord, the soldier, and the teacher. "The absence of higher motives, of common beliefs, which unite and identify people as members of one and the same collectivity, and which discipline and join them together in a common endeavor, had created the crisis." No group was more aware of this perversion of values than the youth of the island, a conviction shared by the alienated intelligentsia.

If the desire to enjoy the advantages of more fortunate neighbors motivates men to change their way of life, then the example of the United States encouraged Cuba—for the Cubans lived next door to an amazingly successful United States. The American miracle as well as American diplomacy for the island, which many Cubans bitterly resented, spurred them to revolution. The achievements of the United States had encouraged a revolution of "rising expectations" in Cuba, while the island repudiated its satellite role within the American political and economic orbit.

Mexico's experience with revolution, in which American foreign policy and business interests had played leading roles, had an important effect on the course of post-1959 Cuban events. In the opinion of Marxists and fellow-travelers who received key jobs in Cuba, the Mexican Revolution was an historical failure and therefore a poor example for Cuba to follow. According to Blas Roca, Mexico had enjoyed a national liberating movement while the Cardenista program of the thirties had influenced the Cuban constitution of 1940, but the Mexican Revolution, which stayed within the confines of a capitalist framework, had fallen into the hands of its American enemies and their Mexican allies, and in the process it had perished. If the Cuban Revolution was to survive intact, said Roca, it would have to avoid the pitfalls into which the Mexicans had stumbled. To build the foundations of a new society, the Cuban Revolution would have to sever the old colonial relationship with the United States which, in Roca's opinion, dictated the socio-economic structure of Latin American society and which the frustrated Mexican Revolution had left undisturbed.

Finally, Cuba had a cataclysmic revolution because its political structure had almost always relied heavily on a national chieftain. From the days of Antonio Maceo and José Martí to those of Batista, Cubans had obediently and often enthusiastically followed such a leader. In Martí, the most famous of these, the Cubans had created a national ideal, a hero to enshrine and worship, both for his philosophy and for the revolutionary leadership he offered in the struggle for independence. In Fidel Castro the Cubans found their latest leader, a bold, politically acute, and charismatic young *caudillo* who claimed that he spoke for the ideals of the immortal Martí.

2.

The Roots of Cuban Nationalism

*Through all of Castro's gyrations, the only constant
has been his determination to free Cuba from
American influence (which he equates with
domination) even at the eventual cost of submitting
his country to the Soviet Union. It was not Castro's
predilection for Communism but his pathological
hatred of the American power structure as he
believed it to be operative in Cuba, together with
his discovery of the impotence of Cuba's supposedly
influential classes, that led him eventually into
the Communist camp. Only from that base, he
thought, could he achieve his goal of eliminating
American influence.*

PHILIP W. BONSAL
United States Ambassador to Cuba, 1959–60

[I]

An aggressive, vocal, anti-American nationalism shaped the
character and direction of the Revolution of 1959.

The origins of Cuban nationalism dated back to nineteenth-
century colonial discontent with Spanish rule. After 1898

nationalist sentiment grew rapidly. According to Philip W. Bonsal, the desire to free Cuba from American tutelage was based on the conviction that "the fate of Cuba . . . was not in Cuban hands." That conviction became the salient feature of the militant nationalism of the first Cuban-born generation of the 1920's. Both Spain and America helped to foster Cuban nationalism, but, of the two, the United States was essentially responsible for the jingoistic nationalism that characterized the Fidelista movement.

[II]

The histories of Cuba and the United States had been intertwined almost from the inception of American independence in 1783. Early American solicitude for Cuba stressed strategic factors. Less than a hundred miles off the Florida coast, Cuba lay in the strategic Caribbean. Cuba must remain in friendly hands. While a weak Spain posed no threat, French or British control endangered American interests. Further, policy-makers in Washington believed that Cuba would fall into their lap if Spain lost the island, and they therefore blocked foreign efforts to liberate the island and frowned on Cuban sentiment for independence.

Prior to the Civil War, the United States had occasionally expressed a desire to acquire Cuba; if this could not be accomplished, the Department of State was content to allow the Madrid government to rule the island. While Southern expansionists wished to purchase Cuba to increase the slave territory of the United States, sectional politics thwarted this aim. A hot debate on the Cuban question continued until the Civil War erupted. The Northern victory at Appomattox silenced the expansionists' cry—though President Ulysses S. Grant made one more half-hearted effort to purchase Cuba. Shielded by the new American military might, Cuba need no longer belong either to Spain or to the United States. It could be independent.

American involvement in the island's affairs continued, however, because a vocal and militant band of Cuban insurgents refused to accept Spanish rule. The bloody Ten Years' War, the first of the struggles against the mother country, erupted in 1868, but unable to vanquish Spain alone, the rebels sought aid abroad, especially in the United States. Americans smuggled arms into Cuba for the insurgents, congressmen voiced their support, and President Grant even suggested that the United States recognize Cuban rebel belligerency. Retaliating, Spain restricted the rights of Americans on the island. In the meantime, lives were lost and millions of dollars of property damaged in Cuba. Washington urged concessions, including the emancipation of the slaves, and eventually compelled a compromise which brought the conflict to an end in 1878. Spain emancipated the slaves, but failed to keep its promise of home rule for Cuba. These half-way measures satisfied no one. Little was done to quiet local demands for self-government, and the bickering between Spain and the United States dragged on until fighting broke out again in 1898.

José Martí opened the final battle for independence in 1895. The United States stayed aloof diplomatically but Spanish attempts to quench the fires of rebellion and Cuban rebel activity in New York and Florida made strict neutrality impossible. A Cuban government-in-exile operated in New York, where Martí made his headquarters, while the Cuban Revolutionary Party solicited funds, recruited men, purchased arms and munitions, and enlisted ship captains for an invasion of the homeland. Spanish consuls in American cities complained that there were Cubans in troop-training centers drilling for the approaching Armageddon, a complaint amply justified later when Martí and his band of fighters landed in Cuba from American ports. All in all, some sixty Cuban expeditions had escaped the vigilance of American officials by 1898. Many of the early patriots acquired American citizenship—and still participated in the battle to free their former homeland. Heading the list of patriots who acquired American citizenship was Tomás Estrada Palma, subsequently first president of the Cuban Republic. Edwin F. Atkins, a sugar planter, noted in his *Sixty Years in Cuba* that nearly all the members of the rebel junta in New York were naturalized American citizens.

No single motive explains the participation of the United States in the Spanish-American War. Popular sympathy for the rebels, Spanish "atrocities," American dreams of world prominence, the need to protect the projected canal across Central America, American interests in Cuba, and the sinking of the battleship Maine—all encouraged American intervention. Of the wars waged by the United States, the Spanish-American proved least costly in lives while only the Mexican War was more profitable. In return for an empire that embraced the Philippines, mid-Pacific islands, Puerto Rico, and Cuba, fewer than one hundred American lives were lost. To Theodore Roosevelt, who undoubtedly voiced the sentiment of his countrymen, "It wasn't much of a war, but it was the best war we had."

Roosevelt's frivolous quip would have angered the Cuban patriots. Cuba had been fighting Spain for nearly three decades and, since 1895, had been engaged in an ugly war with no quarter given on either side. Thousands of Cubans had perished in the bloody conflict to free their homeland; millions of dollars of local property had been pillaged and burned to the ground. To quell the uprising, the Spaniards had herded thousands of Cuban families into vast compounds described by American newspapermen as concentration camps. Cuban historians claim that Spain's retaliatory tactics demonstrate that the insurgents were winning their war and that, in time, they would have defeated the Spaniards had not the United States intervened. No Cuban patriot, insist the historians, asked the Americans to join the struggle; they were uninvited allies.

With Cuba free from Spain, the Americans turned their attention to the job of formulating diplomatic ties with the island and preparing the Cubans for the challenge of self-government. The United States and Cuba were not ready for either task. Ambiguity dictated the American response and the Cubans were politically immature. During the four centuries of colonial rule, they had been given only a limited voice in local matters, and had been without a legislative body of their own until 1897. No sense of social responsibility had motivated either the masters or the colonials. In the absence of self-rule, the Cuban drive for autonomy relied on terror and violence. Further, the Cubans won their independence from Spain despite the protests of local property-holders who predicted mob rule. And some of the insurgents justified their fears. In turn, the Spaniards had sacked the island before departing. Emilio Roig de Leuchsenring, the noted Cuban historian, spoke of a *colonia superviva* that survived the fall of the mother country to frustrate and undermine the dreams of the patriot fathers.

Formal relations between Americans and Cubans began during the era of American occupation of the island. Once the fighting was over, an American military government was established, first under General John R. Brooke and then Leonard Wood, a physician and colonel in Roosevelt's Rough Riders who had earlier supervised United States occupation in Oriente Province. An admiring American scholar declares that Wood "combined sound discipline with a lively imagination" while another compares him to Britain's Lord Curzon as a colonial administrator. A thorough housekeeper and a stern taskmaster, Wood demanded absolute obedience. His political and social accomplishments were impressive: a rural police force to replace the motley band of insurgents;

a reformed judiciary; a system of municipal government; honest and efficient tax collection; separation of Church and State; construction of highways, roads, and public works; and the eradication of disease.

Nevertheless, the occupation spelled trouble. Bickering and misunderstanding between Cubans and Americans flared immediately, for the Cubans quickly strained the patience of their "liberators." Atkins wrote that Americans judged Cubans an inferior and garrulous people who should be taught a lesson. "I hear that the soldiers are exasperated," he said, "and . . . waiting a chance to sail into the Cubans." He reported that many American army officers spoke "plainly about affairs here and are very much disgusted." One American commander concluded that the patriots were "a lot of degenerates, absolutely devoid of humor or gratitude." In the meantime, Atkins and other planters on the island— Spaniards, Americans, and wealthy Cubans—supported the occupation officials. However, the insurgents, who awaited the chance to govern themselves but saw their liberators settle down as conquerors, had their own interpretation. To them—to cite the diplomat, journalist, and gentleman scholar Manuel Márquez Sterling—Wood was the enemy and the occupation a blot on the history of Cuba. This judgment typifies Cuban historical and popular opinion that the evils of the occupation far outweighed the tangible benefits left behind by Wood and his collaborators.

[III]

The occupation over, the Americans left Cuba in native hands —but with a Platt Amendment that permitted Washington to intervene in local affairs. In any attempt to explain the rise of Cuban nationalism, the story of the Platt Amendment supersedes all others. This Amendment, which the State Department and the Senate of the United States imposed on Cuba in 1902, severely curtailed the island's political and economic independence. Further, it encouraged a fear and distrust of the United States bordering on the pathological and transcending the limits of the traditional Spanish suspicion of American motives and policies. One must explore carefully the Cuban's interpretation of the Platt Amendment if only to understand his distrust of the United States and his dream of some day escaping American tutelage, an aspiration shared by his leaders from the patriots of independence to Castro.

Drafted by Elihu Root, Secretary of State in the cabinet of Theodore Roosevelt, the Platt Amendment dictated the norms of Cuban behavior considered proper by the American government. The intent, writes Hubert C. Herring, was "to make . . . [the Cuban Republic] a safe and tractable neighbor." The Amendment limited the authority of the Cuban government to negotiate international treaties and to borrow funds from abroad, and claimed coaling and naval stations on the island for the United States. In short, the Platt Amendment converted Cuba into an American protectorate. "Cuba consents," said one clause of the Amendment, "that the United States may exercise the right to intervene for the preservation of Cuban independence, the maintenance of a government adequate for the protection of life, property, and individual liberty." In other words, the Cubans were told in 1902 to incorporate in their constitution commitments which were diametrically opposed to the Teller Amendment of 1898, in which the American Congress had promised "to leave the government and control of the Island to its people."

The United States abrogated the Platt Amendment in 1934, but scores of Cuban intellectuals and their legion of followers, among them Fidel Castro, neither forgot the humiliation of three decades nor forgave American policy-makers for the misdeeds of their predecessors. The crime of the Platt Amendment, said Miguel Angel Carbonell, was to instill in Cubans a national inferiority complex on the day their Republic was born.

The Platt-Teller contradiction illustrates the ambiguities of the American view of Cuba. United States policy-makers had been of two minds in the days of the Spanish-American War. They wanted an independent Cuba, but with strings attached: the island was free (the Teller promise), but it was also an American protectorate (the Platt Amendment). That contradictory interpretation represented the inevitable result of an historical pattern.

In turn, the Cubans themselves were far from unanimous in their desire for independence, or of one mind on what they wanted of their northern neighbor. In the beginning, they were divided on the question of whether they preferred freedom from Spain, greater local autonomy, or annexation by the United States. To the stubborn patriot, freedom could not be compromised. "Of Spain," to quote the irascible mulatto warrior, Antonio Maceo, "I expect nothing; for Spain has always scorned us; but neither do I hope for aid from the United States." He preferred to fight Spain alone rather than call on his powerful neighbor for help. But according to Edwin F. Atkins, a strong sentiment for annexation pervaded Cuba. In his opinion, the "better class Cubans feared independence," while Leonard Wood, Chief of the American occupation forces, reported that bankers, businessmen, professionals, and clerics demonstrated no enthusiasm for independence. According to Atkins, who is essentially correct in his interpretation, Cuban sentiment on the question of independence split along racial lines. The rebel chieftains who wanted total independence commanded the support of Negroes and mulattos, but a majority of the white property-owners, who looked to American rule for protection, opposed the idea of total independence. In that conflict of opinion the United States was viewed as the potential savior of the whites by one Cuban group and therefore as the enemy of Afro-Cubans by those in the other political camp.

Annexationist sympathies eventually disappeared, yet some members of the old Cuban colonial élite never adopted the Republic as their own. Because annexationist sentiment had a strong appeal in the nineteenth century, it bears closer scrutiny—for the Cuban wish for union with North Americans added another dimension to the Cuban concept of the United States. The role that the United States should play in the island's affairs became an increasingly controversial question.

On the question of union, Cuban feeling reflected the interests of local groups. Before the victory of the North in the Civil War, the question often depended on the issue of slavery, since the native slavocracy was the island's most powerful voice until the late nineteenth century. As long as the Spanish masters permitted the lucrative exploitation of slavery, local planters had little inducement to espouse annexation. But attempts to limit profits, either by American tariff action or a Spanish decision to abolish slavery, rapidly aroused the planters' interest in an alliance with the United States. In the opinion of Ramiro Guerra y Sánchez, author of the monumental *Azucar y Población en las Antillas,* pro-union sentiment reflected the planters' need to preserve slavery on the island in the face of Spanish threats to abolish it. Fearful of the impact free Negroes would have on government and society, the planters sought protection in union. Meanwhile, Cuban foes of slavery generally opposed union with the United States.

After Appomattox, the protagonists reversed positions. Because abolitionists and reformers turned northward for aid and sympathy, annexation became the goal of those who had opposed union before. Among them were many Cubans who, after attending school in the United States, returned home determined to erect a second American paradise on the island. To prevent the growth of this pro-union attitude among students, Spain even banned study in the United States. But annexationist feeling was not confined to the young. Its supporters included a number of notable precursors of independence: Gaspar Betancourt Cisneros, Narciso López and, momentarily, Estrada Palma.

Annexationist sentiment expressed the psychology of a people at odds with their colonial masters, but lacking a clear sense of nationality, of *patria* or *Cubanidad*. True, the annexationist movement was the labor of a relatively small and favored group which, on the whole, lacked ties with the majority of the population. But beyond that, as Guerra y Sánchez concluded, the desire for union with the United States also reflected a strong sense of "national inferiority." Bereft of self-confidence, the Cuban worshipped foreign idols, asking outsiders to provide his economic well-being, his government, and even his culture.

That plea for union with the United States was of native origin, but the Cuban ultimately came to resent the idea and the god he had wooed. The truth could not be expunged from Cuban history, but it was inevitable that intellectuals should later decry that chapter in their country's history. For the ghost of the annexationist movement survived to dampen national ardor long after the dream of annexation faded as a serious alternative. In attempting to live down the past by denouncing the annexationist sentiment of his forefathers, the Cuban nationalist eventually condemned not only his own people but Americans as well.

The role of the United States was more than that of an innocent bystander in the drama then unfolding. In the opinion of Enrique José Varona, the patriot philosopher who joined José Martí in the quest for independence and who became the intellectual mentor of an entire generation, Cuba had been "the obsession of American statesmen" ever since the days when the territorial limits of the United States had reached the banks of the Mississippi River. With New Orleans in their hands and a stake in the Gulf of Mexico and the Caribbean, American diplomats began to deal with the Cuban question as if it were a domestic matter. In their drive for independence, therefore, Cubans had to recognize that the United States and not Spain alone had an interest in their plans for the future. Cuban historians stress that this interest became self-evident after the United States blocked the Mexican-Colombian project to free Cuba in 1823.

Prior to that time, Cubans had looked to Spain and, on occasion, to their sister Spanish-American republics for a settlement of their political status. After the United States interposed itself, informing the patriots that it expected them to live under Spanish tutelage, the insurgents concluded that the answer to Cuba's future could be found only in Washington. But their attempts to win freedom there brought no positive results until the South was defeated in the Civil War. American policy favored Spanish rule on the island, or a union of Cuba with the United States. The decision to work for a settlement of Cuba's political status through the United States proved judicious only after Washington accepted the idea of a free Cuba, envisaged in terms of a protectorate and a commercial alliance. But again, to cite Varona, the United States held the trump cards, a fact no Cuban could ignore.

It should not be concluded, however, that Cuban reactions to American intervention in the battle against Spain were consistent. They veered in unpredictable ways, especially in the years immediately following independence. Cuban attitudes ranged from moral approval of intervention to violent, outraged rejection of the American role in 1898.

In general, Cuban attitudes reflected the political beliefs of the time. Conservatives frequently expressed approval of American military intervention in 1898, while liberals were hostile. But the exceptions make this generalization risky. Ultimately, however, pro-interventionist sentiment virtually disappeared and, regardless of politics, Cubans rarely defended the American intervention of 1898.

Cuban opinion on the Platt Amendment offered no unanimity of thought, for that opinion embodied not merely condemnation of American intervention in 1898, but diverse Cuban views on the importance of independent, domestic leadership. Conservative businessmen, sugar planters, and those Spaniards who remained in Cuba after 1898, most of whom favored close ties with their neighbor to the north, generally took a dim view of the concept of total independence for Cuba. The fall of the Estrada Palma administration in 1906 led these Cubans to advocate a strong American supervisory role in Cuba. In their opinion, Cubans lacked the preparation for self-government—as the collapse of the Estrada Palma administration demonstrated. To avoid costly and bloody civil strife, Cuba needed American advice and supervision. Further, the Platt Amendment's stress on law and order encouraged foreign investment, without which, they believed, there was no bright future for Cuba. Peace, stability, and economic development came in a capsule, with the Platt Amendment. Thus, in terms of practical politics, the Conservative Party voiced less criticism of the Platt Amendment than the Liberal Party, which was usually hostile. But given the "apolitical" nature of local politics, opinion on the Platt Amendment did not always mirror party loyalties.

In a similar manner, intellectual opinion on the Platt Amendment and on American foreign policy for Cuba ranged from acceptance to ambivalence to outright hostility. Few Cuban intellectuals defended this policy, but some fatalistically accepted the inevitability of America's role in Cuba. Enrique José Varona even convinced himself that Cubans should be grateful to their liberators because American soldiers had fought to break the shackles that bound the island to tyranny. A peaceful, orderly, and progressive Cuba, the product of commercial and diplomatic ties with the United States, would mean the triumph of American political ideals on the island. True, said Varona, the United States occupied Cuba, but the occupation originated in the inability of the Cubans to vanquish Spain alone. In addition, American intervention prevented the Spaniards from laying waste the island and thus saved Cuba for civilization. In Varona's opinion, the Americans arrived in Cuba as the spokesmen for Cuban independence and, after Cuban independence was won, departed from the island. As a reward for their contribution and their interest, Americans deserved a place in the Cuban constitution: logic demanded that they impose a Platt Amendment. To deny the American stake in Cuba or to think of Cuba as an isolated island in a far-off corner of the world was unrealistic. Cubans must embrace American tutelage willingly and happily, for the United States was their benefactor. In turn, the United States had a moral obligation to guarantee the peace and progress of Cuba. Since liberty and justice represented the goals of both peoples, the Platt Amendment, which promised to make the goals a reality, discouraged conflict between the two countries.

Opposed to Varona's interpretation was a view which laid the blame for American intervention on the doorstep of those Cubans who failed to live up to their share of the bargain. In the opinion of the veteran diplomat, Cosme de la Torriente, local malpractices compelled the United States to invoke the Platt Amendment improperly—responsibility for "prostitution" of the Amendment rested on Cuban shoulders.

At another extreme stood popular opinion of the Platt Amendment. To the majority of Cubans, the Amendment was the *coyunda insoportable*—the yoke of colonialism. The phrase expressed all the rancor and bitterness of a suppressed people. Through no choice of their own, Cubans had lost the right to rule themselves. America had cast itself in the role of tutor, and its interference, charged historian Herminio Portell-Vilá, inevitably favored weak, corrupt, and tyrannical Cuban regimes, never the popular will. No matter what went awry, Cuban politicians could always blame the United States. Had Cubans been left to their own devices, they could have recognized their own mistakes and worked to create a free and independent society.

Portell-Vilá and other Cuban historians denied that the chronic political problems of the pre-1934 era were uniquely Cuban, claiming they were common to all emerging nations —even to the America of George Washington's time, as the events of the Whiskey Rebellion demonstrated. Cuba's difficulties furnished proof not of incapacity to govern but of political inexperience, which only self-rule could provide. Nor was revolution, that cardinal sin to the fathers of the Platt Amendment, a subversive idea, for, given the character of Cuban politics, revolution represented the essence of democracy. In a land where elections meant little, how were the people to change their government? To deny the right of revolution was to build a wall between the politicians and the people, blocking the possibility of achieving a free society.

The Platt doctrine ignored that truth, while at the same time offering the Cubans a facile way out of their domestic difficulties. But reliance on the United States eventually engendered among Cubans a loss of faith in their Republic and in their own nationality. As the poet and critic Felix Lizaso noted, Cubans could not resolve their own problems without fear of outside interference. Thus the ideal of nationality was weakened and corrupted by the self-indulgent nature of politics and the tarnished reputation that captive institutions acquired in the popular mind. Anything that favored the propagation of the ideal of nationality, of *Cubanidad*, which by implication refuted the Platt doctrine, Cuban intellectuals judged patriotic. The net effect of United States interventionist diplomacy was moral and psychological. The Cubans saw themselves as a captive people, Lizaso concluded, and the Platt Amendment as a limitation on their liberty. That, and not the actual loss of political rights, was the crux of the problem.

The State Department's proclivity to define loosely the Platt Amendment aggravated the situation. The Americans, Cuban critics charged, converted a pledge to safeguard local institutions into a policy to protect American investment— from the Cubans themselves and from outside competition. If intervention was indeed inevitable, said these Cubans, the United States could at least obey the letter of its own commitment which, as defined by Elihu Root, was "not synonymous with intermeddling or interference with the affairs of the Cuban government." To cite the sociologist-historian Fernando Ortiz, whose *Contrapunto Cubano del Tabaco y del Azucar* in English translation is read widely in the United States, the commitment did not endorse illegitimate, incompetent, and sanguinary government in Cuba.

At no time was the intensity of Cuban resentment of American diplomacy exhibited more fully than during the Constitutional Convention of 1901, which debated whether to include the Platt Amendment in the national charter. Despite Washington's instructions, which warned the Cuban delegates that their only choice was to endorse the Platt Amendment, a prolonged and acrimonious struggle split the delegates into two camps. Neither group backed the Amendment, but the majority recognized that Cuba must either bow to the American fiat and thereby win limited independence, or reject it and continue under foreign military rule. The minority was prepared to fight on until "victory or death."

In the end the Cubans ratified the Platt Amendment because no alternative existed, but an agonizing debate and two votes were necessary before the inevitable prevailed. The first vote carried by a majority of one (fifteen to fourteen) with two delegates absent. Cuban historians believe that the absent members planned to cast negative votes, but did not want to lend their names to the tragic farce. So, while grown men, many with tears in their eyes, voted in favor, others bearing some of Cuba's most illustrious names cast negative votes. After the vote one delegate, General José Lacret, enshrined his name in Cuban history by shouting: "Cuba is dead; we are enslaved forever"—a sentiment that undoubtedly expressed popular feeling. But worse was still to come; for the Cubans modified the Platt Amendment before voting and hedged on their promise to accept it. Washington promptly rejected their version and compelled them to meet again. This time, by a vote of sixteen to eleven, the Platt Amendment was added to the Cuban Constitution.

No Cuban nationalist has ever forgotten that humiliation. On the eve of independence, the Cuban had confronted truth: in theory he was a free man, but in practice he was a vassal of the United States. It was out of such experiences that Cuban attitudes toward the United States evolved.

The Cuban had to live with the Platt Amendment for three decades. The debate over the Platt Amendment plagued politics until 1933, for all political parties took a stand on the doctrine. In his campaign against Estrada Palma in 1901, General Bartolomé Maso had privately condemned the doctrine but dared not make his views public, fearing, according to some Cuban historians, American reprisals. To combat the Platt Amendment Cubans founded a number of organizations. In 1909 a Liga Antiplatista was established in Havana; the Sociedad Cubana del Derecho Internacional, which dated from 1915, carried on an unrelenting campaign against the doctrine. These were the forerunners of many groups that in one way or another attacked "the humiliation of 1901."

Abroad, the Platt Amendment dogged the Cuban diplomat's footsteps, a constant reminder of his country's colonial status. The Platt Amendment was particularly galling to Cuban pride at international gatherings. In the eyes of foreign diplomats, the politician-diplomat Carlos Márquez Sterling asserted, Cubans were only half-independent, citizens of a country with limited rights. To no one's surprise, therefore, Cuban diplomats worked diligently to erase this blot on their nation and, in so doing, invented ingenious interpretations to circumvent the Platt dictum. That of the senator and jurist José Manuel Cortina, which defined the Platt Amendment as "contractual" in character, deserves special attention.

Cortina presented his thesis in a pamphlet entitled *Ideas Internacionales de Cuba,* in which he rejected the assumption that to accept the Platt Amendment as a bilateral contract was to formalize Cuba's dependent status. The reverse was true, he said: since the Amendment was an international agreement sanctioned by the legislative bodies of two countries, to endorse it was to guarantee and strengthen the island's independence. Cortina's purpose was to invert the terms of the Platt Amendment, to give international recognition to the fact that any actions which infringed upon or destroyed the independence of Cuba were based on a false interpretation of the doctrine. If the goal of the contract was to maintain Cuban independence, and if Cuba had endorsed the doctrine with that understanding, violation of that independence was tantamount to violation of the Amendment.

Cortina's ingenious interpretation was but one of numerous attempts to circumvent the Platt Amendment. That the influential Senator, a spokesman for the sugar industry which stood to gain from the industry's ties with the United States, should have joined the critics was no surprise to students of Cuban affairs, for the Platt Amendment, by restricting sovereignty, created a psychological problem felt deeply by every Cuban, regardless of his politics. To be free of the Platt Amendment and thereby of the United States was the na-

tional dream. The poet Enrique Hernández Miyares expressed
that sentiment when he wrote:

> Upon my return from distant shores
> With my saddened soul in mourning,
> Solicitously I looked for my flag . . .
> And saw another flying beside it!
>   Where is my Cuban flag,
> The most beautiful flag of all?
> This morning I saw it from the ship,
> And I have never seen a more sorrowful thing!

*   *   *   *   *   *   *

> Although I see it flutter sadly and limply,
> I live for the day when the sun, in all its brilliance,
> Will illuminate it alone—alone—
> On the plains, on the seas and on the peaks of mountains!

The Platt Amendment left an indelible imprint on the
Cuban mind. From the day it was imposed on Cuba, no
Cuban was free to choose the path of his country's future.
He felt himself bound to the United States, a conviction that
survived even the abrogation of the doctrine. Whether justified or not, he convinced himself that he lived at the mercy
of his powerful neighbor. As the Cuban sociologist Fernando
Ortiz has noted in *El Deber Norteamericano*, the Cuban
found himself irresistibly drawn to the subject of the island's
ties to the United States, and to what should or could be done
to alter or improve them.

Individual responses emerged in a kaleidoscopic pattern,
said Ortiz. Some Cubans attempted to get Washington to
modify its policies, others wooed United States investors in
order to obtain the material benefits of American progress,
while others sought a treaty of commercial reciprocity.
Cubans of different sympathies joined hands with American financial interests to exploit their fellow-Cubans—

spending millions of dollars on propaganda to mask their motives. Some tried to persuade American intellectuals of the need to support Cuba's right to self-determination. Others asked Washington to intervene diplomatically or militarily to prevent or to uphold political change in their homeland. In summary, said Ortiz, Cubans openly or indirectly accepted American tutelage, uncompromisingly opposed that tutelage, or learned to live with it without losing their sense of personal dignity or engaging in polemical denunciations —making, therefore, the best of a bad situation.

[IV]

Whether by accident or design, during the Platt era Cuba fell into the hands of politicians friendly to America. Estrada Palma, the first president of Cuba and a long-time resident of the United States, is remembered by critics for his desire that Americans "guarantee" the internal peace of his country. A politician of the Moderate Party, Estrada Palma won the presidency with the support of the well-to-do in his campaign against General Maso, a Liberal and the popular choice. As President, he acquiesced to American demands for naval and coaling stations, but fortunately for Cubans, the United States occupied only Guantánamo. That base alone, nevertheless, kept alive friction between the two countries.

Estrada Palma enjoyed three favorable presidential years, then plunged himself and the United States into difficulties. Honest and well-intentioned but vain and ambitious, he re-elected himself in 1906 despite protests of the Liberal opposition. Civil strife erupted immediately, but Estrada

Palma refused to compromise, confident that the Americans would rush to his rescue. Unable to quell the Liberal revolt that burst out, he invoked the Platt Amendment and asked the United States to intervene. President Theodore Roosevelt hesitated momentarily but, when Estrada Palma reported that rebels threatened to burn and pillage foreign property, sent troops to Cuba. Estrada Palma then resigned, leaving Roosevelt to solve the problem. So began the years of intervention and the use of American troops as an alternative to confronting issues which, if handled properly, might have led to political stability.

To restore peace and order, Roosevelt sent William Howard Taft, his Secretary of War and a presidential hopeful, who arrived in Havana in September 1906 and left early in October—delighted to have rid himself of the Cuban problem with his political reputation still intact. His successor was Charles E. Magoon, a midwestern city politician who spoke no Spanish and who ran Cuba as if it were Chicago. A tireless worker who wanted to please, Magoon granted "hundreds of petitions a day, entertained lavishly, and ironically," remarks Hudson Strode in his *Pageant of Cuba,* "achieved a contemptible reputation which very nearly wiped out the excellent impression of American administration. . . ." Cubans remember Magoon for his offers of well-paying jobs with nominal duties—the notorious *botellas,* "nursing bottles full of rich milk for the political babies." He launched a gigantic public works program for the unemployed and built 600 kilometers of roads—more than the Spaniards had constructed in four centuries—but Cuban and foreign entrepreneurs made immense fortunes on public-works contracts.

International difficulties between the United States and Cuba were in the embryonic stage. From 1909 when Magoon left the island in the care of the Liberals, until 1933 when the structure assembled in the days of the Platt Amendment collapsed temporarily, the United States acted as the arbiter of Cuban affairs. In 1912 American troops helped to quell an uprising in Cuba—over the protests of President José Miguel Gómez; and four years later American troops again landed in Cuba—in answer to a plea from President Mario García Menocal (1912–20), who had studied in American schools, earned a degree in engineering from Cornell University, and managed the largest of the Cuban-American Sugar Company properties. García Menocal's frauds in the 1920 election compelled Washington to intervene once more and to appoint a State Department adviser for the incoming Cuban administration.

President Alfredo Zayas (1920–24) had to contend with General Enoch Crowder, sent by the Woodrow Wilson administration to unravel the Cuban tangle. Crowder told Zayas what to spend, lectured him on the necessity for public honesty, and selected an "honest cabinet" for him. Shorn of real authority, Zayas found himself depicted in a Cuban newspaper cartoon, pen in hand, asking: "Which name shall I sign, Crowder or Zayas?" The Cubans, meanwhile, split into groups of "interventionists" and "noninterventionists." Interventionists—the minority—believed the transformation of Cuba's structure would come only with American advice and consent, while noninterventionists— vociferous critics of the Platt Amendment—opposed Crowder and condemned American "meddling" in Cuban affairs. Faced with a financial crisis brought on by the collapse of the sugar bonanza, Crowder solved Cuba's difficulties by borrowing from New York banks. Ultimately, Zayas shook himself free of his protector, but not of the public debt left behind by his policies.

Until 1933 American policy under the Platt Amendment was relatively unhindered in Cuba, for few of the Cuban leaders or parties, after all, had really voiced the sentiments of the people. The State Department, its representatives in

Cuba, and American troops and warships had usually arbitrated quarrels between rival bands of politicians. The American interventions had wounded the national pride of a minority of Cubans, albeit the most literate and public-minded; but the net effect of two decades of such practices was to encourage the growth of a sense of nationalism among a larger and larger segment of the population. By the late 1920's the people disturbed by the role of American diplomacy in Cuban affairs which, in their opinion, had prostituted local politics, included not merely intellectuals and the militant nationalists of the past but students, professional men from socially prominent families, and countless members of clandestine labor organizations. Strong critics of the Platt Amendment, the new nationalists demanded not only the transformation of Cuban society, but a radical alteration in the island's ties with the United States. Nothing less would satisfy their aspirations.

American policy under the Platt Amendment, more than any other single factor, was responsible for both the rise of the new nationalism and for much of its anti-American tenor. The era of limited Cuban protest to intervention, sanctioned by the Platt Amendment, ended with the struggle against the dictatorship of Gerardo Machado, the man elected to succeed Zayas. A protector of American investment in Cuba, Machado received both diplomatic and financial support from the United States until his downfall in 1933.

3.

Sweet and Bitter

The bank that underwrites the cutting of the cane is foreign, the consumers' market is foreign, the administrative staff set up in Cuba, the machinery that is installed, the capital that is invested, the very land of Cuba held by foreign ownership and enfeoffed to the central, *all are foreign, as are, logically enough, the profits that flow out of the country to enrich others.*

FERNANDO ORTIZ

[I]

In the three decades of American political domination of Cuba, businessmen and capital from the United States won virtual control of the Cuban economy. Meanwhile, the framework of the economy was permanently fixed. In sugar, Spain had supplied the basic ingredient, but a mechanized sugar economy, intimately linked to the American market and the offspring of American capital, dictated a unique non-Spanish development. Cubans were of many minds concerning the plant and its American patrons who had transformed the island into the "sugar plantation of the world."

For sugar, that delight of foreign and native consumer, proved a bitter sweet. In its benevolent moods, it fostered prosperity and progress, but suffering, despair, and hunger were the fruits of its wrath. The patriot fathers, many Cubans believed, never intended that their descendents be enslaved by sugar. Their ideal was an autonomous Cuba. In the view of the historian Herminio Portell-Vilá, who has left his harsh verdict on the pages of countless articles and books, a fundamental incompatibility existed between the colonial sugar industry and the dream of independence. The patrons of nationalism had frowned on the "parasitical industry"; none had envisaged a Republic wholly dependent on sugar. Yet the plant was crowned monarch of the island. How it came to be—an old, complicated, and controversial story—almost always involved the activity of Americans. That story, and the evils of the sugar industry, helped to produce the Revolution of 1959.

[II]

The early facts are immutable. Sugar arrived on the island in the sixteenth century, legend claiming that Columbus brought the cane stalks on his second voyage. In climate and land, Cuba proved ideal for the cultivation of cane, but a limited market in Europe, the scarcity of cheap labor, and the cost of equipment and transport retarded production for nearly two centuries. Then, in 1789, Negro slave uprisings erupted in neighboring Haiti which forced French planters to flee the island, leaving behind a plantation economy in ruins. Haiti had been a major sugar supplier for the European market, which now faced a shortage. As the price of sugar rose, the Spaniards stepped into the breach. In Cuba virgin lands were planted to cane, often by small farmers whose fields quickly overran the livestock ranches of the old but small colonial élite. By mid-nineteenth century there were thousands of small sugar farmers. Thus, in the beginning, sugar proved a welcomed tonic for the stagnant colonial economy of Cuba.

But subsequent events transformed that providential beginning. In the 1870's European beet-sugar producers began to threaten the monopoly of cane-planters, and sugar prices went into another period of decline, reaching a new low by the 1890's. Large, competitive producers survived the hard times, but the need to grow and mill cheap sugar eliminated inefficient producers, the small farmers. Of the approximately 1,500 mills which had produced sugar in Cuba during the 1850's, only 400 remained in 1894, and less than half of these weathered the changes wrought by independence. Meanwhile, the annual production of sugar rose from 300,-000 tons to a record crop of 5.9 million in 1925. The surviving mills expanded rapidly, demanding additional cane from the large planters, who planted more land to cane. American capitalists provided funds to expand the mills and to satisfy their hunger for cane. By 1925 the requirements of cheap sugar had imposed on the formerly sleepy island an agro-industrial wage economy of huge mill-complexes (centrales), renter planters (colonos), and seasonal labor. The ownership and operation of this new sugar system were largely in the hands of American bankers, managers, and technicians.

Many Cubans watched the boom apprehensively as crop after crop shattered old production records and the octopus-like centrales spread their tentacles over the island. In the 1920's the lands reserved for cane monopolized more than half of the island's tillable surface, while tobacco, that ancient and venerated Cuban staple, occupied only a fraction. Land was needed for fresh plantings, for the gardens, roads, and railways of the *centrales*, to protect the water supply of the plantations, and to lie fallow, reserved for the day when the land presently cultivated would be exhausted. The reserve nearly equaled that planted to cane. And as early as 1911, lamented Enrique José Varona, foreigners owned and controlled the finest lands. A decade later Ramiro Guerra y Sánchez predicted "the economic ruin and the social and economic decay of the country" unless Cubans checked the growth of the sugar latifundia. More radical critics, writes the politician and commentator Mario García Kohly, demanded an immediate solution in the Mexican manner: expropriation of the huge estates and subdivision of their lands among small farmers.

The *colonos*, an intermediate class of planters who contracted to plant, cultivate, harvest, and deliver cane to the mills, formed one of the major props of the sugar structure. Nearly all Cuban historians uncritically censure the *colono* system, but its development was not an unmixed evil. The system gave many former slaves an opportunity to enjoy relative independence, to have land to till, a product to sell, and a sense of personal responsibility. Meanwhile, more prosperous *colonos*, almost always white men, even hired labor for their lands—just as the giant plantation-mill complexes did. However, a majority, approximately two out of three, tilled mill lands in 1930. These *colonos* were vassals of the mills, which advanced them funds to cover operating costs during the planting and growing season, and thus their prosperity depended on the well-being of the mills.

Cheap sugar demanded low production costs, which slave labor helped provide until the abolition of slavery in the 1880's. After that, most of the former slaves—for only a fraction became *colonos*—joined the growing horde of seasonal laborers, fieldhands who worked for wages. Further, Negroes from Haiti and Jamaica, Mexican Indians from Yucatan, and Chinese were imported to meet the demands for cheap labor of the sugar barons, who claimed that the *guajiros* would not work. Critics replied that cheap labor lowered wages in the sugar industry, driving local labor from the scene. *Guajiros* would not work for the low wages which seemed adequate only to the exploited Negroes. "I will not cut cane; let the wind do it," was the sentiment of the *guajiro*. At the end of the harvest, most of the immigrants from near-by islands returned home, but many stayed, darkening the racial picture and heightening racial tensions, which further divided local society along ethnic lines. In the twenties, however, changes in the sugar industry drove whites as well as native Negroes and mulattoes to labor in the cane fields.

Rural Cubans were wage-workers and farmers who produced for a market; there was virtually no subsistence farming. The economics of sugar decreed that man work only part of each year. Jobs were plentiful in the dry season from December until the April *zafra* or harvest, and almost nonexistent in the rainy months, the *tiempo muerto*, except in boom years when there were lands to clear and plantings to make. In the old days, before the use of modern machinery, the *zafra* had continued for nearly four months. New techniques and mechanization changed that; by the 1920's Cubans were milling record crops in half the time. Cuba produced more sugar but provided fewer jobs.

Climatic factors aggravated the picture still more, since the demand for labor followed the tempo of sugar. Hiring in the tobacco industry coincided with the *zafra;* the coffeeberry picking time varied only slightly; while potatoes, malangas, yuccas, tomatoes, and lima beans were harvested during the same period. Even the tourist trade was on a similar schedule, for two-thirds of the visitors arrived in the spring. The impact on the economy of these seasonal factors was disastrous. Periodic unemployment plagued commerce and industry as well as agriculture, which employed more than half the labor force. The island, in effect, suffered from chronic, seasonal, and cyclical unemployment.

Cuba had built a lopsided export economy, in which foreign consumers determined the degree of prosperity on the island. The Cuban complained that he was at the mercy of forces outside his control: foreign tariffs, quotas, business cycles, wars, and technological changes. In nearly every respect, the island was a vast sugar latifundia, where today and tomorrow revolved around the sale of sugar to foreign buyers and where little independence or security existed for the worker. An international banking agency reported that one of the major barriers blocking domestic development was the lack of confidence of Cubans in their country, which stemmed in large measure from the shaky nature of the sugar economy.

Reliance on the export of sugar distorted the economy in another way. Despite its unpredictable market, sugar had often smiled on Cuba. Countless Cubans had reaped a rich reward as the sugar planters of the world. Businessmen, importers, and politicians believed that sugar would be perpetually kind to them. Men with capital to branch out into other crops invested in sugar, while the growing of food was left to small farmers who lacked funds, equipment, and knowledge. The sugar barons who ruled the island favored their product and extended few benefits to the farmers who produced food; in fact, attempts were made periodically to keep food prices down. Cubans, therefore, imported most of their food. Nearly all the rice consumed locally came from abroad, half of the beans and the meat, though much of island's land was in grass and pasture. Hog farming

was a haphazard enterprise. Eggs and poultry were purchased in foreign markets. Tomatoes, green peppers, cu-
cumbers, and okra, all grown locally, were exported.

Sugar, a jealous and domineering master, set the pace
of life. When the rains fell and plant life awakened, man
had almost nothing to do; this was the *tiempo muerto,*
sugar's growing season. Only a minority of workers had
jobs in the mills. In the fall, the island bestirred itself. Mills
were repaired and the hunt for workers began. With the
opening of the *zafra,* the whole island came alive. There
were millions of tons of cane to be cut by thousands of
workers, who jammed the roads and highways on their way
to the fields. The unemployed now had jobs and money to
spend. Families that ate raw cane during the summer months
clamored for rice and cooking oils and liquidated debts
accumulated during the dead season. The money they spent
injected new life into the national economy. All segments
of society benefited: wholesalers sold more because the
village grocer paid his bills; stevedores loaded the sugar on
ships that carried it to foreign ports; and bankers and businessmen supervised and financed the gigantic operation.

The early decades of independence proved a windfall for
Cuba. Compared to Africans and Asians, and the majority
of Latin Americans, the Cubans were relatively well-off.
However, a more careful scrutiny, which Cubans were beginning to make, inevitably revealed serious flaws. The
majority of rural and urban workers enjoyed a thin slice of
the prosperity; their lot was just slightly better than that
of the poor in other lands. They were ill-fed, ill-housed,
poorly schooled, and indifferently governed. After the Great
Crash of 1929 brought the economy to its knees, the critics
decided to transform the structure which, in their opinion,
had betrayed Cuba.

[III]

Economic ties between the island and the United States had begun in the nineteenth century. Geography and climate, and a Spain too backward to supply the island with basic necessities or to consume its products, determined that Americans play a prominent role in Cuba. By 1850 the United States was the leading consumer of the island's produce. From that date, insists Fernando Ortiz, Cuba was an economic colony of the United States. On the island, the production of sugar for the American market superseded all other activity. But until the Spanish-American War, the planters were Spaniards and Cubans, although adventurous Americans had already infiltrated their ranks.

Independence transformed the sugar industry, and that transformation encouraged the final struggle for independence. As Ortiz and others have testified, the sugar industry developed rapidly in the last decades of the nineteenth century, above all by relying on an expanding market in the United States. On occasion, Spain attempted to discourage this growing dependency, but never seriously, for all parties profited—Spain as well as local planters. Raw sugar enjoyed a free American market until 1893. Then the Wilson Tariff, a response to the economic crisis that engulfed the United States, raised duties on imported sugar. As Cuban profits dropped, discontent swept the island; sugar-planters who had previously opposed national autonomy began to consider it. The Wilson Tariff kindled the fires of independence. According to Edwin Atkins, insurrection on the island coincided with tariff legislation in the United States that adversely affected the market for Cuban sugar. High tariffs and the hard times that followed in Cuba, he pointed out, spread the spirit of rebellion to all groups. It was logical, therefore, that one of the patriot fathers of Cuban independence should be Tomás Estrada Palma, a sugar-planter.

The Platt Amendment, which protected the island from the danger of civil strife and property damage which had discouraged foreign investment earlier, drew Cuba and the United States closer together. With the protection of the United States and the guarantees offered by the planter-oriented rulers of Cuba, the entrepreneur could invest his funds safely. Businessmen with an eye to investment in Cuba received additional encouragement in the Reciprocity Treaty of 1903, which granted Cuban sugar a tariff reduction of 20 per cent in the American market—in return for preferential tariff rates of up to 40 per cent for American goods in the Cuban market. Stability and reciprocity stimulated business on the island and investment from abroad, chiefly from the United States.

Cubans as well as Americans were the beneficiaries. The Cubans had jobs and a measure of prosperity as American capital and technology developed the island. Foreign investors joined the island by rail, linking the eastern provinces with Havana, while others poured their capital into mining. Americans smoked more than half the Cuban tobacco sold abroad, and the profits went to Cubans, many of them small farmers who used their dollars to improve the quality and production of their staple.

More lucrative boom days befell Cuba during World War I. As the price of sugar rose, more American capital entered the island. Forest lands were cleared and planted to cane and more Negroes imported from the Antilles to provide cheap labor. The conflict in Europe finally ended, but prosperity continued. From February to May of 1920, Cubans whirled in the frenzied "Dance of the Millions," as sugar prices spiraled skyward, ultimately reaching the fantastic price of 22.5 cents a pound. As if by magic, speculators and planters made tremendous fortunes overnight. In Ha-

vana ecstatic millionaires built palatial mansions on $100,-
000 lots that no one had wanted a few months before, joined
lush new country clubs, and made tennis and golf national
pastimes.

Then sugar prices fell to 3.58 cents a pound and the
boom faltered, the victim of world overproduction, specula-
tive credit policies, and the Emergency Tariff Act in the
United States. But outwardly Cuba recovered its prosperity
by 1923, aided partly by a loan from J. P. Morgan and
Company and, more important, by a brief revival of the
market for sugar and the dollars of American tourists seeking
whiskey, fun, and sun in Cuba after the Volstead Act banned
liquor in the United States. Unfortunately for Cuba, world
overproduction, including bumper crops at home, again
pulled sugar prices down in 1926. This time the precipitous
decline continued unchecked. In 1932 the wholesale price
of sugar dropped to less than a cent a pound.

Prosperity and the economic catastrophes of the twenties
accelerated the transformation of the Cuban sugar industry,
altering sharply the local economy. In their haste to share
in the bonanza, Cuban-owned mills, planters, and *colonos*
had borrowed funds to expand operations; the financial
crises caught them unprepared to meet their obligations
while, unprotected by adequate reserves, the local banks
which had provided the credit went bankrupt. Foreign
capital stepped into the breach, buying up local properties
and extending even further its control over the island's resources and the Cubans themselves.

American interests established an iron grip on Cuba. From
$200 million in 1914, American investment climbed to $1.2
billion by 1923, half of it in sugar. Refineries in the United
States acquired Cuban mills and millions of acres of fertile
lands. In 1908 Cuba supplied a tenth of the world's sugar;
in 1920 the figure reached 25 per cent, more than half of
it produced by American-owned corporations. Exports from

sugar-cane products jumped from 54.1 per cent of the total national export to 88.6 per cent. Life on the island rested almost exclusively on the export of sugar cane, much of it owned by American corporations, and the bulk of it sold in the United States.

The Cuban had succumbed to a striking historical irony: in winning his limited independence, he had lost control of his economic resources. Before the influx of American capital, Cuban and Spaniard were masters of their own house. In the countryside, most of the land remained in native hands, and land ownership, despite the existence of slavery, was widespread. Any enterprising Cuban or Spaniard, explains Leland H. Jenks, could become a planter, borrowing money from the local bank, purchasing land and a small mill, paying the labor from his sales, and liquidating the mortgage with his profits. The emergence of giant mills shattered the idyl. Such mills were costly to build and operate; even wealthy foreigners lacked sufficient capital. Corporate enterprise, foreign-owned and managed, provided temporary relief, but the modern sugar industry demanded capital and credit beyond even its resources. Eventually, the demand for long-term financing drew big bankers onto the scene, who granted new loans to protect their original investment. Some purchased property outright or acquired it through foreclosures. A stock-buying American public financed the operation. And so, charged Ortiz, a foreign plutocracy of banks and financial companies established itself as master of Cuba.

The financial stake modified the Cuban diplomacy of the United States. As American capital poured into the island, Washington shifted its emphasis from strategic considerations to the protection of United States property. Behind this shift loomed American special interests, which demanded a voice in the island's political affairs commensurate with their investment. As the American investor saw it, the wealth of the island was largely his, but he had no vote in the government. It was, to quote Atkins, "a question of taxation without representation." To safeguard his property, the American businessman demanded the protection of his government, but any move by Washington to heed that demand further limited Cuba's political independence.

The Cubans, in the interim, were left to wrestle with their faltering economy, to devise formulas that would restore and stabilize it. Ultimately, they had to accept blueprints which further involved powerful American interests and which dictated, in an attempt to raise prices, the amount of sugar cane to be planted and sold. As hostile Cubans interpreted them, such plans sacrificed national welfare to the interests of native and foreign sugar magnates. None of them, not even the grandiose Chadbourne Plan of 1930, coped effectively with the problem; although Cuba reduced the amount of sugar it produced, the expected world decline in sugar production never materialized. Instead, neomercantilist policies spurred importing nations to produce their own sugar behind tariff walls. The effects were disastrous. In 1933, wrote Luis Machado, an adviser to the American Chamber of Commerce in Cuba, hundreds of thousands of jobless men hunted fruitlessly for work. Mounting political unrest followed in the wake of unemployment.

[IV]

Cubans who censured the role of the sugar industry had one basic complaint. Most national ills, according to them, stemmed from the nature of the industry and its reliance on the United States for survival. In their judgment, the maladies were endemic to the system, as old as the Republic. In accepting sugar as a copartner of political independence, the early rulers of Cuba had wasted a golden opportunity to root out a growing evil. The industry was then in its infant stage, though its tentacles were already threatening to overrun the entire economy. But the patriot armies had laid waste the industry, pillaging and burning mills and cane fields. In the opinion of Portell-Vilá, the backbone of the plantation had been broken; the sugar industry lay prostrate. The misfortunes of sugar offered the opportunity to halt its growth and to reconstruct the industry in answer to national needs, but Cubans had not taken advantage of that opportunity.

Instead, occupation authorities did everything possible to stimulate the recovery and growth of the sugar industry. Wood and his subordinates, however, not only revived the industry, but made certain that the island would remain tied to American capital and markets. To quote Portell-Vilá, the United States "shored up and reestablished for its own benefit the system that had been overthrown." No one consulted those insurgents who urged a different form of economic development.

Further, the commentators charged that the capital brought into Cuba had imperiled the task of building a nation. The influx of dollars arrived, explained Alberto Lamar Schweyer in *La Crisis del Patriotismo*, before Cubans had had the necessary time and unity to build a nation. Weak ideologically, they had put personal gain above the national welfare and, to keep their ill-gotten wealth, had betrayed moral and spiritual values and fallen prey to American capital. The Cuban experience, concluded Lamar Schweyer, was an example of what wealth could do to a people unprepared to use it wisely. And, lamented Felix Lisazo, as the Cubans had acquired wealth, they had isolated themselves from their intelligentsia, the group most concerned with the moral and spiritual health of Cuba. In the end, concluded a member of that intelligentsia, José Antonio Portuondo, American wealth created the "bitter days of the frustrated Republic."

Foreign capital, to summarize this argument of the hostile critics, had seduced the Cubans. The attempts of foreigners to subjugate the economy of Cuba to their whims, said Fernando Ortiz, colored the entire history of the sugar industry. From the days of Charles V and his Fugger bankers, foreign capitalists had waged an unrelenting battle for mastery of Cuba and, in the end, they had conquered. American corporations dictated decisions; Americans owned the major mills; American banks underwrote the expense of cutting and milling cane; and the market for sugar was American. Americans had transformed Cuba into a vast plantation exploited for the benefit of Americans.

Cuba, stressed Ortiz, would never be truly autonomous until it shook itself free of "the coils of the serpent of the colonial economy that fattens on the fruit of Cuba's soil but strangles the Cubans," converting their "coat of arms . . . into the sign of the Yankee dollar." The lopsided colonial economy, Varona added, forced the country to import basic necessities. But only Cubans could correct these absurdities, warned Guerra y Sánchez, for the American profiteer would not attack his source of income.

Not all Cubans, however, condemned the nature of the sugar industry or wanted to limit the American role on the island. Support for the status quo ranged from that of the Unión Social Económica de Cuba, the Cuban Chamber of Commerce, the Rotarians and Kiwanis, to that of influential importers. In their opinion, the structure of the sugar industry was essential to the welfare and survival of the Cuban economy. The prosperity of the industry, and by implication that of the nation, demanded strong bonds between Cuba and the United States. Occupation officials had behaved prudently when they had protected and favored the development of the sugar industry. In the view of spokesmen for the Unión Social, "natural" law dictated that countries in geographic proximity, which produced different products and complemented each other, trade with one another. To ignore this axiom would saddle both neighbors "with a heavy loss of wealth"—as past instances of such folly demonstrated. The Unión Social denied that Cuba was "a foreign country for the United States"; rather, Cuba "occupied a peculiar and exclusive position for the American people." The Unión Social declared that Cuba was an economic adjunct of the United States because of the peculiar interrelationship that stemmed from the sugar trade between the two countries. To upset that arrangement would be to court disaster.

The view that the United States determined Cuba's welfare, an interpretation that accepted frankly the status of Cuba as a colony of the United States, had the approval of a majority of those in the middle- and upper-income brackets. But, paradoxically, many of them questioned the wisdom of the relationship—as a cursory glance at their writings makes clear. Their conviction that Cuba had no future outside the sugar economy, but that the arrangement left them at the mercy of their capricious neighbor, placed these Cubans on the horns of a dilemma. The fact that ruling groups accepted their colonial position in no way denies the truth that they were deeply troubled by the urgent need to sell their product on the American market.

The majority of the Cuban people, who had no voice in policy-making, expressed no unanimous or inflexible opinion. His job, the amount of his take-home pay, and the welfare of his family largely determined the attitude of the worker. In times of full employment, he seldom questioned the wisdom of national policy, yet in periods of unemployment he proved a willing disciple of the agitator and reformer who blamed national woes on sugar. Since unemployment was a chronic evil, however, the sugar question remained a constant topic of conversation and worry among the workers. Cubans in every walk of life, therefore, gave a disproportionate amount of their attention to the sugar problem, and to the Americans who participated in the industry as investors, managers, and customers. That the United States purchased the bulk of Cuban tobacco, vegetables and fruits grown for export, and supplied the machinery for domestic industry, further helped to remind Cubans of their colonial status. In brief, whatever Cubans believed about economics, politics, or international affairs, they were highly sensitive on the subject of sugar and, concomitantly, on the nature of their relationship to the United States.

No question disturbed Cuban critics more than the latifundia system spawned by the sugar industry. The debate over the land problem began with the birth of the Republic. In 1903 Manuel Sanguily, one the insurgents, introduced in the Cuban congress a bill to forbid the sale of land to foreigners, in the belief that the evils of the latifundia were of foreign origin. Cuban intellectuals, whose writings on the subject are prolific, quickly took up Sanguily's criticism. Although it became fashionable to pin the radical label on these critics, most of them were moderates of orthodox economic views. Of course, leftists lent their voices to the protest, but so did conservatives, as well as labor leaders, students and university professors, and small farmers and *colonos* who coveted corporation-owned lands. Outside of the landowning minority and its political allies, a majority of Cubans were disturbed by the inequality in the pattern of land ownership and, particularly, by the amount of land in foreign hands. Through the attention they gave to the problem, scholars such as the renowned Guerra y Sánchez built their reputations.

The question was what to do about the land problem, an

issue that involved American control and ownership of huge tracts of land. The reformer's efforts to find a solution to the problem, moreover, confronted him with an unpalatable truth: because Cuba's prosperity depended almost entirely on the sale of sugar to the United States, to reform the landholding pattern would undoubtedly jeopardize that prosperity by antagonizing the American investor and the State Department. Nearly all proposed reforms equivocated, therefore, and stopped short of urging expropriation and subdivision of the large estates. Most plans simply suggested that farmers be given public lands or, in extreme cases, the corporation-owned lands lying fallow. However, reformers acknowledged that even these mild proposals could not be enacted without the consent of American interests and their government in Washington—if Cuba was to maintain fruitful economic and political relations with the United States.

The price of sugar on the American and world market also kept the sugar question firmly in the limelight. In response to the laws of supply and demand, the price often fluctuated from season to season, despite attempts of producers to control the supply. Although the United States had granted Cuba a quota and had fixed prices, the price of sugar invariably rose in wartime and dropped precipitously with peace, while sugar producers prospered in eras of scarcity but agonized when nature made possible bumper crops.

In essence, therefore, the question was how to reduce or manipulate production to keep prices up. Unfortunately, Cuban economists, sugar producers, politicians, and reformers never found the answer. National thinking ranged from elaborate production and marketing schemes to laissez-faire remedies. Washington's quota and price system helped immeasurably, but since the Cuban supply always exceeded the American quota, the quota system offered only a partial solution.

The Cubans therefore found a convenient scapegoat in American tariff policy, in the producers of beet- and cane-sugar in the United States, or in what they called "Wall Street." The problem, as seen by such critics as Portell-Vilá, could be reduced to the constant plea for preferential treatment for Cuban sugar on the American market, for which Cuban sugar interests were prepared to sell their souls. These souls, he reminded his readers, which the sugar barons and their allies were willing to exchange for a share of the American market, were the Cubans themselves.

On one point the Cuban critics of the sugar industry stood in agreement: immediate and effective steps must be taken to regulate the industry and its foreign allies. The critics differed only on how to do it. Some simply urged the modification of the system, a replacement, in the words of Guerra y Sánchez, of the "ruthless methods of commercial exploitation" with "just and reasonable" ones. The palliative, he warned, must not take the form of an attack on "the sugar industry, or . . . domestic and foreign capital." The evil lay not in the crop itself or in foreign capital, but in the exploitation that characterized the system. No reason would exist for complaint once the people owned and tilled their own sugar lands.

More radical Cuban critics, however, believed that control was not the answer to the problems of the sugar industry. They condemned the excessive Cuban reliance on sugar, the system itself, the flow of foreign capital into their country, and the role of United States diplomacy in Cuba. Many of these critics spoke out in the late twenties and lent their voices to the chorus of protests that culminated in the revolution of 1933, the forerunner of the Fidelista movement of the fifties.

4.

José Martí

Thus, Martí is no longer merely the creator of independence; he is, in addition to that, the soul of the nation, the living gospel of the fatherland. His image is the model, to the extent that any evaluation of the Republic's history should begin by asking whether or not it has kept faith with his teachings. The martiano is the just, the disinterested, the useful. The oblique, the greedy, the futile is the negation itself of Martí, of his renovating death.

FRANCISCO ICHAZO

I carry in my heart the teachings of the Maestro. Martí is the instigator of the 26th of July Movement.

FIDEL CASTRO

[I]

The revolution that toppled Gerardo Machado in 1933 discovered its intellectual mentor in José Martí and, as Fidel Castro justly claimed, twenty years later furnished the intellectual leadership for the 26th of July Movement. In their views of Cuban society and of the United States and its economic and political policy in Cuba, both Castro and the revolutionaries of 1933 reiterated the ideas of Martí, the patriot philosopher and politician. In this respect, Castro and the revolutionaries of the thirties walked in the mainstream of Cuban thought which had enobled Martí as the prophet. No one occupies an analogous place in the history of the United States. It would require a composite of Washington, Jefferson, and Lincoln, supplemented by the best of Henry James, Emerson, and Twain to suggest a comparable figure.

Since the twenties, Cuban leaders of all political parties and of every major political and intellectual movement had offered homage to Martí. Machado, the dictator of the decade, made his public tribute; his enemies, the Auténticos who ultimately deposed him, took their name from the claim that they spoke as the "authentic" disciples of Martí; Batista, who betrayed them, said he acted in accordance with the wishes of Martí. In his book on Martí, Richard B. Gray discusses the opinion of a Havana school teacher that Martí's dreams of a "better government in Cuba" had inspired the majority of the youthful opponents of Batista's regime. Every Cuban intellectual, noted Martí's distinguished biographer, Gonzalo Quesada y Miranda, had either written a book or an article on Martí, or planned to do so. Among Martí's admirers stood Castro who, according to Teresa Casuso, had published essays on Martí, and whose early ideas relied so heavily on Martí's writings that Batista did not allow him to read Martí's works when he was jailed in the summer of 1953. In his famous speech, *History Will Absolve Me*, in which he justified his part in the Moncada attack, Castro cited or referred to Martí ten times.

The Fidelista claim of speaking for Martí survived the military phase of the Revolution and became a public assertion of the revolutionary regime. To paraphrase Ernesto Guevara, who undoubtedly shared Castro's intimate thoughts, the Fidelistas had resurrected the movement that Martí led in behalf of Cuban independence and that American intervention destroyed. Castro declared that his socio-economic blueprints for Cuba expressed the ideal of *humanismo*—a direct reference to Martí's thesis that *patria* and *humanidad* were synonymous. The government, said President Osvaldo Dorticós, had to remind the Cuban people "again and again, today and every day," that the ultimate goal was to convert Martí's dreams for Cuba into reality. At the Punta del Este Conference in 1963, which condemned Cuba's alignment with the Communist bloc, Dorticós defended his country's policy on the ground that it obeyed the teachings of Martí.

Martí was an eclectic who borrowed from a multitude of sources; he was the Aladdin of both huckster and patriot. Widespread devotion to Martí stems, as the scholar-politician Jorge Mañach recognizes, partly from the profusion of his writings, in which he became "all things to all men." Culling the Apostle's writings for his ideas is a herculean task. At best, one can find what one considers representative, but always with the recognition that more appropriate selections or even, as Mañach notes, contradictory ones, might be chosen. In Martí, according to a 1930 editorial in *Bohemia*, the Cuban people discovered "the human synthesis of its finest sentiments, of its dearest desires, of its highest destiny." To probe Martí's writings, therefore, is not merely to discover Cuban thought in all its complexity, but the basic ideas that inspired the Cuban revolutionaries of the thirties and Castro.

Foreigners may find it difficult to sympathize with the Cuban worship of Martí, for nothing stamps his life more than failure. From the time of his birth until his death in 1895, Martí suffered a life of heartache and despair, of plots that collapsed or were thwarted prematurely. In truth, Martí was a martyr to his love for Cuban independence, a fanatical devotion that transcended normal human behavior, providing a role he obviously relished. (Castro, too, thrives on conflict;

he invites attack. "I have the honor," he once said, "of having been the target of the roughest, most continuous and most infamous attacks.") Martí was not a typical man, and certainly not in the North American sense, in which nonsuccess and tragedy often symbolize negative qualities. Perhaps it is this sense of failure, this picture of the idealistic Martí as a victim of the inevitable, that endears him to Cubans.

Martí and his teachings left a profound mark on the youth of Cuba. The cult of Martí is the creation of the first republican-born generation of the twenties, fervent idealists, reformers, and nationalists who gave the cult form and substance. Until then, Martí's ideas lay dormant though not forgotten. In Martí, the restless and frustrated generation of the twenties discovered a symbol. The revolt against Machado climaxed the effort of a Martí-inspired generation, hungry for the Cuba that the martyr had envisaged before his death.

[II]

Martí, the man and the cult, epitomizes Cuban pride in self and country. Yet, in the manner that has characterized so many of the island's thinkers, Martí was as much the offspring of the United States as of his native land. He loved and idealized Cuba, but his ideas were conditioned by long years in the United States, a country whose intellectuals shaped many of his thoughts but whose politicians and diplomats he feared and distrusted.

Born in Havana in 1853, Martí—like Castro—was the son of Spanish immigrants who settled in Cuba. While he was still in school, the Ten Years' War, the first of the "struggles for Cuban independence," broke out. Martí, like other youths of the time, drank freely of the heady wine of independence and was soon writing and distributing seditious anti-Spanish literature. The Spaniards took a dim view of his activities and in 1870, when he was just seventeen, sentenced him to six years of hard labor in a rock quarry. He served only a few months of this sentence, then was banished to Spain, where he continued his schooling at the universities of Madrid and Zaragosa, receiving degrees in law, philosophy, and letters— subjects Castro would study later.

In 1874 Martí left Spain for France, then departed for Mexico (where Castro spent his exile years), and Guatemala. After the Pact of Zanjón in 1878, which ended the Ten Years' War, Martí returned to Cuba. His political activities on behalf of Cuban independence, however, quickly involved him in difficulties with the Spanish authorities and he was again banished in 1879. After a brief stay in Venezuela, Martí settled in New York, where he made his home until 1895. In Mexico he had married Carmen Zayas Bazán, a Cuban, who bore him a son, but the marriage proved unhappy, and, separated from his wife, he acquired a mistress in New York, by whom he had a daughter. Supporting himself by working as an art critic for the New York *Sun*, he spent his years in exile plotting the independence of Cuba.

As a typical first-generation product, Martí possessed an undying loyalty to the land of his birth. Yet he spent only a fraction of his adult life in Cuba. From 1881 until just before his death in 1895, he never left America, where he won prominence as a Cuban patriot and thinker. In the United States, writes the Mexican Andrés Iduarte, Martí became a propagandist, politician, and man of action. Of the seventy-four volumes of his collected writings, seventeen discuss life in the land of his exile.

Martí worshipped heroes, among them, American writers and thinkers. His supreme hero was Ralph Waldo Emerson, about whom he wrote his finest literary essays. Martí prized

Emerson's Americanism, his love for and faith in the democratic life. He highly esteemed Walt Whitman, whom he called the poet of the people. Had Martí published in English, and had he not been Cuban, Felix Lizaso believes, Americans might have looked on him as the last of the transcendentalists. Martí had an excellent grasp of Henry James, while the ideas of Washington, Jefferson, Hamilton, and Lincoln, as well as the works of historians William H. Prescott and George Bancroft, figured prominently in his political philosophy. Martí thought well of Wendell Phillips and was a close friend of Charles A. Dana, editor of the *Sun*, in which he published frequently.

Fidel Castro, on the other hand, spent only a few months in the United States but, during his conspiratorial days, worked closely with Cuban exiles in American cities who were plotting the fall of the Batista regime. Castro, who reads and speaks English, also carefully studied American political literature. In *History Will Absolve Me*, he supported a key argument with a quote from the Declaration of Independence, paying especial tribute to one "beautiful paragraph": "We hold these truths to be self-evident, that all men are created equal . . . ." Castro knew the passage from memory!

Martí did not cut a new path for Cuban intellectuals and patriots. Others had preceded him, including the illustrious trio of patriot thinkers whom Mañach has called the "forefathers of Cuban national consciousness": Father Felix Varela, José Antonio Saco, and José de la Luz y Caballero. Varela, earliest of the insurgent intellectuals, left Cuba in 1821 and eventually settled in the United States where, among his diverse activities, he translated into Spanish Thomas Jefferson's *Parliamentary Manual*, nearly became a bishop in New York City, and worked diligently for Cuban freedom. His disciple, Saco, journalist, sociologist, and author of the distinguished six-volume *Historia de la Esclavitud*, spent part of his exile years in America. Luz y Caballero, who visited the United States, was a student of Longfellow, Ticknor, and Prescott, while acknowledging a sincere admiration for the American historical school.

Students and followers of Martí, many of whom played decisive roles in the battle for independence or figured in the political life of the early Republic, also learned from the American scene. Their number is legion: Enrique José Varona; Manuel Sanguily, poet, intellectual, and fighter for independence; the scholar and politician, Fernando Ortiz; Jorge Mañach, the Harvard-educated intellectual whose *Martí, El Apostol,* ranks as a classic in Cuban literature; Cosme de la Torriente, the diplomat; and Herminio Portell-Vilá. Among the intellectuals and disciples of Martí they represent but a sampling of those who came to know their North American neighbor intimately.

Like Castro, Martí was essentially a politician. Much of what he wrote and did reflected the politician's ambivalence, his preoccupation with the practical. He contradicted himself, taking on occasion positions which conflicted with his objectves; for example, seeking arms in the United States for a Cuba he promised would be free of both Spanish and American influence.

In his formative years, Martí seems to have been a romantic idealist, an interpretation that Castro would later not merely accept but defend. "To those who would call me a dreamer," said Castro, "I quote the words of Martí." Then, between 1883 and 1887, Martí altered his thinking; the decisive year was 1886. (Castro had altered his political thought by 1961, rejecting humanism for Marxist-Leninist doctrines.) Martí read widely, becoming more thoughtful, liberalizing his outlook on social, economic, and political issues. His early writings censured labor unions, criticized their attacks on management, and defended the monied classes. By 1887 he had rejected these views, becoming an ally of worker and reformer. Martí's pro-capitalist, anti-labor, and pro-American essays characterize the period that ends in 1883.

What induced this transformation? No single answer provides a satisfactory explanation. In attempting to explain this shift in Martí's thinking, most of his students stress that he became progressively disenchanted with the United States. His haven was the nation of the Gilded Age, the industrial society of the Robber Barons, of the Vanderbilts, Rockefellers, and their political lackeys. In its callous disregard for human suffering, the Gilded Age alienated the Cuban, a man who lived from hand to mouth and who felt injustice deeply. His life in the slums of New York sharpened his interest in social questions. The transformation in his thinking crystallized in the Haymarket Square riots of 1886, which he reported in terms sympathetic to labor. Martí, the man of action and the reformer, emerged in the years after 1886. In his subsequent writings, therefore, the earlier contradictions tend to disappear.

Martí was a pugnacious nationalist and fighter for Cuban independence, a cause which both he and Castro viewed as a morally sanctioned goal. ("To be Cuban," says Castro, "implies a duty, and to evade it is treason [because] the lives of all of us are joined forever to this idea and to this future; we do not want to live without a country. . . .") It would be difficult to exaggerate Martí's nationalist ardor. He spoke of the war against Spain in terms of a crusade against evil— much as Castro did in his attacks on the Batista administration. The supreme sacrifice that Martí preached was to die for Cuba. He denied Cubans the right to put personal interests above the national welfare, for only *patria* mattered. "He who loves the fatherland cannot think of himself," he wrote a few days before his death. Some scholars believe that Martí may have deliberately invited death at Dos Ríos, where the Spaniards killed him in battle. He resented any criticism of Cuba. In his famous reply to an article in *The Manufac-*

turer of Philadelphia which censured Cubans for their failings, he passionately defended his countrymen, their struggle for independence, and their valor. Martí's nationalism, his defense of Cuban values, and his willingness to find fault with America help explain the revived interest in him in the 1920's. In Martí, the nationalist, reform-minded critics of Cuba's dependence on the United States discovered a kindred soul.

Castro enjoyed his role as an anti-Batista revolutionary, but not more than Martí relished his struggle against the Spaniards. To Castro, to use Teresa Casuso's description, the Cuban revolution was a mistress. To Martí, the revolution for Cuba's independence was a religion. In his last interview, with a reporter for the New York *Herald* in Cuba, Martí voiced the conviction of the revolutionary that those who opposed his dreams of a free Cuba were nothing but parasites, traitors, and *gusanos* [worms]—an expression which Castro now employs to denounce his enemies. No grounds for compromise existed with the opposition. Martí admonished: "You take your rights, you do not beg for them; you do not buy them with tears but with blood." Despots relinquished their power to those who destroyed them, never to those who knelt before them. Revolution signaled the coming of an epic stage in man's history, of a new life emerging out of the clash of contradictory and conflicting opinions. (For Castro, "the right to rebellion lies at the very roots of Cuba's existence as a nation.") To compel the Spaniards to grant Cuba independence, Martí in 1895 landed on the eastern shore of the island and fled inland to join insurgent guerrilla bands that awaited his arrival. Four decades later, Castro and his followers reenacted Martí's plan of battle in the same Sierra Maestra.

Although Martí did not sire the Cuban revolutionary tradition, he enhanced it, giving that tradition the mantle of glory which later revolutionaries employed to justify their activities. Nearly all of Martí's adult life, seventeen of his forty years, dealt with revolution. To cite Iduarte, the revolutionary and Martí were brothers. Castro, the revolutionary, and Martí, therefore, share a common background.

In addition, Martí's revolutionary gospel had a populist slant similar to Castro's. *Patria* spelled *humanidad,* a blend of humanitarianism and humanist beliefs that led Martí to preach that man could and should vanquish the moral and social afflictions of society. He saw the rural people, the urban workers, the Indians, and the Negroes as heirs apparent of the reformer's efforts and the bulwarks of an independent Cuba. "I will stake my fate on the poor of the earth" was his favorite saying. (Castro: "When we speak of struggle, the people means the vast unredeemed masses, to whom all make promises and whom all deceive. . . .") Martí's essays on the Haymarket Square riots and on the philanthropist Peter Cooper reveal a heartfelt compassion for the underdog. Until his death Martí was a spokesman for racial equality, deploring all forms of discrimination, calling for assimilation of the Negro into Cuban society, and alleging that the whites exploited their dark-skinned brothers—arguments Castro employs regularly. Martí warned that the white man's fear of the Negro and his belief that freedom from Spain would leave him at the mercy of his former slaves had wrought untold harm to the cause of independence. He preached a racial democracy in which men, regardless of color, would be equal in fact as well as in theory—a radical doctrine in nineteenth-century Cuba. Since Negro and mulatto made up the greater part of the Cuban working force, his racial thesis had broad socio-economic implications. Any program to improve their welfare would transform the structure of Cuban society.

Martí's revolutionary faith led him to reject the Church. In the tradition of Spanish-American reformers of the nineteenth century, Martí, though Catholic by birth and upbringing, discarded his formal religious beliefs, much as Castro—the child of Catholic parents and the product of Catholic schools—rejected the Church and chose for his Bible the doctrines of Marx. In his *Hombre del Campo* and other writings, Martí ccnsured the Church, particularly the rural clergy, for its neglect of the social welfare of the poor. He admonished Cubans to think for themselves, not "to respect the priest, because he will not permit you to think." Martí admired Benito Juárez, whose reforms in the Mexico of the 1850's deprived the Church of its special privileges. As a Mason, he engaged in anti-Catholic activities for which the Church excommunicated him.

Martí's anticlericalism, combined with his advocacy of reform, has persuaded many leftist scholars and some Marxists that Martí was either a Marxist or neo-Marxist. Antonio Martínez Bello, for example, developed the thesis (in *Ideas Sociales y Económicas de José Martí,* 1940) that Martí was a Marxist in all but name, that his ideas and those of Marx rested on common assumptions and had similar goals. Another Marxist scholar, the historian Emilio Roig de Leuchsenring, holds a corresponding opinion. Both Roig and Martínez Bello stress that Martí and Marx held the same views on labor and urged workers to band together to demand and protect their rights. According to Roig, Marx urged the workers of the world to unite, while Martí prescribed "solidarity" for "our people."

Martí undoubtedly sympathized with many of Marx's tenets, for his obituary on the German pays tribute to Marx's compassion for the welfare of the worker. In principle, says Iduarte, Martí stood shoulder to shoulder with Marx. It does not follow, however, that Martí was a Marxist or a Socialist either by conviction or temperament. His empathy with Marx, as Mañach perceives, sprang from a humanitarianism unmarred by dogma. Juan Marinello, a noted Marxist and

Martí scholar, has demonstrated convincingly that Martí was not a disciple of Marx. Marinello pictures Martí as a romantic whose views differed "directly and indirectly, from the key assumptions of Marx"; yet he claims that Cuba's Socialist Revolution has kept faith with the ideas of Martí. The contradiction in Marinello's analysis is more apparent than real, however, because Martí (as Iduarte concedes) thoroughly disliked professional anti-Marxists; he reserved his enmity not for the reformer who instigated social progress, but for his enemies.

Those Marxists who think they discover a companion-in-arms in Martí do so for the simple reason that nearly anyone can find his particular moral or social philosophy in Martí's writings. Like the Castro of 1959, Martí had no fixed political philosophy. In a broad, Latin American sense he was a typical middle-class thinker reminiscent of the Castro who, on turning Socialist in 1961, described his earlier career as that of a "political illiterate."

Yet Martí's endorsement of liberty, justice for the working man, and racial equality should not be equated with a commitment to Western democratic principles. Despite his long residence in the United States and his admiration for Emerson and Whitman, he revealed no clear grasp of democratic institutions or attitudes. On the contrary, one suspects that Martí either misunderstood or opposed democracy as Americans know it—much in the manner that Castro, who voiced apparent commitments to democracy, later modified or rejected them.

Martí's equivocal interpretation of liberty supports the above analysis. He put special stress on liberty as an ideal, but asked his followers to obey unreservedly the dictates of the nation-state which, in his opinion, superseded the rights of the individual. Unrestrained individual freedom frightened Martí, but he spoke glowingly of public service and of the citizen's duties to his government. Gray believes that Martí employed the concept of liberty to rally Cubans behind the cause of independence, but would have restricted liberty once independence had been won. In Gray's opinion, Martí would have promptly substituted duty, patriotism, and obedience for liberty and democracy.

In the pattern of the Cuban revolutionaries of today, Martí was the victim of his logic. Until the type of government the revolutionary advocates wins power, the goal is resistance; once that government is installed, the protestor of yesterday, confronted with the "true wisdom" of today's leaders, becomes a traitor. It is important to remember that Martí frequently expressed contempt for "common spirits" and admired the strong men of history. He spent his formative years in Cuba, Spain, and Spanish America where *caudillos* ruled with an iron hand. He condemned them, yet, as a product of their society, he could hardly have escaped their baneful influence. Moreover, Martí thought of himself as a great political leader, and while it is true that such men can learn to become democrats, they seldom do so in Spanish American countries.

Three documents embody Martís political ideas: the *Resoluciomes*, the *Bases del Partido Revolucionario Cubano*, and *Manifiesto de Montecristi*, each written for a specific purpose and published between November 28, 1891 and March 25, 1895. Martís letters to Federico Henríquez y Carvajal and Manuel Mercado shed additional light on his ideas. None of the documents contains a detailed political blueprint, or promises a specific political system. None calls for a constitution. (In this respect, Castro broke with Martí—in his *History Will Absolve Me,* he demanded compliance with the Constitution of 1940, a demand he quickly ignored once in power.) Politics was "a resolution of equations to Martí," Gray states, an attempt to maintain a state of equilibrium among various groups in society. In his writings Martí justified the absence of a detailed political program, on the basis that local needs would determine the nature of the Cuban government. In

Nuestra América, furthermore, he cautioned Cubans not to copy foreign political systems, declaring specifically that the Cuban people could commit no greater error than to imitate political practices born of a completely different experience in the United States.

Martí's economic concepts were equally vague. His ideas were orthodox—in so far as he possessed any knowledge of economics. He accepted the classical liberalism of the nineteenth century, but believed that national wealth flowed from agriculture, not from industry—a thesis Castro accepted after 1963. Unlike most Latin American thinkers, Martí eulogized manual labor, tilling the soil with one's own hands. He hoped to end Cuba's growing reliance on sugar (Castro's early goal) and advocated crop diversification to avoid the evils of monoculture. "A people commit suicide on the day that they come to rely on one product," Martí believed. Martí promised land reform: "The path to progress in Latin America lies in the redistribution of the land."

Martí held public education in high esteem. He stressed the need to educate lest the people be "deformed like the monster of Horace, with a huge head and heart, but with tiny arms of skin and bones." But Martí deprecated the "mistaken" emphasis on urban and traditional schooling, urging that Cuban schools teach the practical subjects of scientific agriculture, mechanics, physics, and chemistry—a belief Castro shares.

[III]

In his opinions on the United States, Martí shared a common Cuban ambivalence. His praises of the United States were legion, yet no Cuban—not even Fidel Castro—has ever surpassed Martí in his denunciations of American life. His writings include scores of essays describing the negative quality of life in the United States and his fear that Cuba would one day fall victim to American expansionism. José Enrique Rodó, whose *Ariel* became the Spanish American testament on the United States, took his critical interpretations of North American culture from the writings of Martí.

The political and economic realities of the Western Hemisphere, in which the United States enjoyed a virtual hegemony, shaped Martí's essentially negative view of that nation. In his opinion, geographical proximity had placed Cuba at the mercy of the United States. He admitted that a special relationship existed between the two peoples and acknowledged that Cuba's independence required American benevolence or neutrality. Yet, as Castro ultimately maintained, Martí believed that Cuba should not court the aid of the American government because that aid would restrict and compromise its freedom. Further, Martí warned against adopting an economic system that would invite American political domination, arguing that economic union meant political union. No nation has true autonomy, to cite Martí, if it sells only to one buyer, because the seller can not fix the terms of trade. In his writings on sugar, Martí maintained that no truly autonomous nation had ever relied on the cultivation of a single crop for export to a single market. Nonetheless, though Martí opposed direct American intervention in Cuban affairs and condemned the role of American sugar interests in Cuba, he assiduously courted public sympathy and official benevolence in the United States. While he wanted a Cuba without entangling alliances, he never intended to make an enemy of the United States, warning that unfriendly relations would prove disastrous. But friendship, he emphasized, should never lead to political or economic subservience; Cubans must have the moral courage to act independently of the great powers.

In a manner typical of a majority of Cubans and Latin Americans, Martí judged North Americans by a double standard. He admired individual Americans, and proudly accepted their friendship, but distrusted America as a nation. He feared particularly the opinions and policies of American bankers and businessmen, but reserved his invective for James G. Blaine and his school of politicians, whose venality and self-interest he flayed.

Martí insisted that Americans neither knew nor understood Cuba. Unable to read or write Spanish and without a knowledge of its history or culture, Americans lacked insight into Cuban character and motives. Because of their peculiar relationship to Cuba, however, Americans had to know the island. Thus Martí spent much of his life in exile discussing the nature of Cuban culture and civilization and explaining the movement for Cuban independence.

Yet Martí's writings reveal that he was skeptical of his ability to persuade Americans of the justice of his cause and that he placed little faith in their friendship. No one, Martí concluded, could "expect charity or friendship" from the United States, a nation which he believed had risen to prominence at the expense of its neighbors while spreading the doctrine of Anglo-Saxon supremacy. "These colossal ruffians," he wrote in *Esquema Ideológica,* "rely on the tactics of the prize-ring and, only recently liberated from their jungle past, live for politics." In his often-quoted letter to Manuel Mercado, written a few days before his death, Martí declared he would happily sacrifice his life if that act would stop the advance of the United States into Hispanic America. "What I have done and what I will do is for that end." To quote his famous phrase: "I have lived in the bowels of the monster and I know it."

[IV]

Martí thought of himself as a spokesman for all Latin America. Like Castro, who has participated in a Colombian revolution, engaged in vendettas with Venezuelan leaders, and advocated grandiose economic-aid programs for Latin America, Martí made Latin America his arena of interest and activity. At various times he was consul for Uruguay and Argentina, North American correspondent for a chain of South American newspapers, and in 1889 served with the Uruguayan delegation to the first Pan-American conference. In the performance of these roles and in his capacity as chief of the Cuban independence movement, Martí had much advice to offer his Spanish American neighbors. That advice never included support for the American doctrine of Pan-Americanism—which Castro also has condemned.

Two distinct peoples, Martí warned, which language and psychology had set poles apart from each other, inhabit the lands of the Western Hemisphere. Martí's America spoke Spanish, worshipped non-Protestant gods, and struggled to win an independent existence. He cautioned Latin Americans not to send their children to study in the United States because he feared American wealth would suborn the young and impressionable, encouraging them to cast aside native values and look down on their countrymen. Hispanic America had not broken its colonial bonds merely to become a captive of North American imperialism. Martí did not support alliances with the United States against Europe nor with Europe against a Western Hemisphere nation, insisting that the geographical proximity of North and South Americans should not lead to a union of the two peoples. Hispanic America, he said on the occasion of the Pan-American conference of 1889, spoke for the collective welfare of its people.

[V]

Castro may have deliberately adopted and followed the ideas of Martí, or he may have accepted them because they were commonly held beliefs in Cuba. Whatever the explanation, Castro and the 26th of July Movement stepped out of the mold created by the independence struggle that Martí led more than a half a century before. The writings of Martí certainly inspired those youthful leaders of the revolution that toppled the Machado regime in 1933, a revolution that repudiated three decades of Cuban history and development closely identified with the American role in Cuba.

5.

The Lost Opportunity

*Motherland Muse, this is not
What Martí wished for.*
      AGUSTIN ACOSTA, *La Zafra*, 1927

[I]

The year 1933 marked a momentous change in the history of
Cuba, in which the protest and discontent of the twenties and
the disillusionment with the results of independence united
to produce a revolution that toppled the dictator, Gerardo
Machado, and promised to institute vital reforms in Cuba.
The product of youthful enthusiasm and "middle-class" leadership, the revolution offered the island an opportunity to
redress old grievances and to build new socio-economic foundations in an evolutionary, nonviolent manner. Unfortunately for Cuba and the United States, nothing came of the
opportunity and the day of reckoning was postponed until
Castro instigated an armed rebellion that surpassed in method
and goals the moderate aspirations of the revolt of the
thirties.

[II]

Cuban historians remember Gerardo Machado as the despot who betrayed public confidence. Yet Machado, undoubtedly the popular choice for president, had prevailed over his opponent on his promise to put an end to the moral turpitude of the Zayas and the Menocals. His failure to live up to public expectations lit the fires of the 1933 revolution, which many Cuban critics view as the logical successor to the thwarted struggle for independence. Before the revolution subsided, it had threatened the island's socio-economic foundations and therefore its traditional ties with the United States.

Machado was a distinguished patriot and veteran of the independence wars who, after an initial, unsuccessful fling at politics, retired to the business world where he acquired a reputation for ability and efficiency. He was reportedly incorruptible. As a candidate for the presidency, he committed himself to providing the people with "water, roads, and schools." He offered his countrymen, recalled Alberto Arredondo, the regime that Martí had envisaged: "Cuba with and for all." In the beginning, Machado did not disappoint his backers; his regime invested millions of pesos in eye-catching public works projects, while his face-lifting program won the plaudits of many who judged him "a man who accomplished what he preached." In a much-discussed speech, the Archbishop of Havana pontificated that paradise had "God in Heaven and Machado in Cuba."

In 1926, convinced by his legions of enthusiastic followers that he was Cuba's indispensable man, Machado had a compliant Congress extend the presidential term of office and designate him the national executive for another six years. But he had the misfortune of ruling in an era of falling sugar prices. To stay in office, he began to employ an iron fist and, as his old admirers deserted him, to stifle protest with his pampered army and gang of hired killers. Hard times, which had shaken the anemic economic structure since 1926, cost him whatever support he claimed among urban and rural workers.

Machado had assumed office in an era of great expectations, in the years known as the period of Cuban revisionism, of the national debate over the social, economic, and political ills of Cuba. In Europe the Russians had recently implanted a new social system, while a revolution in neighboring Mexico had swept aside a regime rooted in the colonial past. Agrarian reform programs characterized both revolutions. To the young and the reform-inclined, and to an increasingly larger number of Cubans convinced that their native land suffered from agrarian ills, the two revolutions stirred hope for change. The reform spirit even reached Machado's collaborators. From the desks of Luis Machado, Celso Cuellar, Gustavo Gutiérrez, and Antonio Antón there flowed an unending series of blueprints for agrarian reform, but Machado ignored them all.

In his election speeches, Machado had offered the voters two specific pledges: to bring about the long-awaited moral regeneration of government and to fight for abrogation of the Platt Amendment. But he proved to be no more nationalistic than his predecessors. A patron of American business and banking interests, he voiced no further criticism of the Platt Amendment and, disregarding nationalist sentiments, financed his graft-ridden administration and his public works projects with loans from American bankers. Washington, meanwhile, acquiesced to the inevitable by recognizing Machado's dictatorship and, until 1933, Havana and Washington were on the best of terms.

In the interim, the United States harvested the enmity of Machado's foes, who believed America kept Machado in office because it condoned his political improbity, provided him with financial backing, and closed its eyes to the injustice that gripped the island. The national protest against Machado, therefore, was not limited to him and the society he symbolized, but was also directed against the Cuban diplomacy of the United States, its businessmen on the island, and their control of the sugar industry.

[III]

The anguish of the era centered in the youth of Cuba. The first republican-born generation had come of age in the twenties, and inherited a Cuba in crisis. Economic difficulties had destroyed the prosperity of the sugar industry, while corruption and cynicism too often characterized the political structure. The idealism and hope of Martí, idol of the new generation, had vanished from the political scene. It was time, said the youth of the island, to restore the faith of the Apostle.

Machado vented his ire on the National University of Havana, focus of unrest and intellectual discontent, for both teachers and students censored the dictator. He closed the University after professors complained they could not teach with soldiers in the classrooms. Shortly afterwards, Machado shut the doors of every high school and teachers college. But his repressive tactics backfired. Before long the students, led by the Directorio Estudiantil Universitario, were holding clandestine meetings and plotting the downfall of their antagonist. Their manifestoes, which they distributed by the carload, demanded not only a change in government, but a "moderate social revolution" that would free Cuba of "foreign domination." The manifestoes stressed five points: abrogation of the Platt Amendment; revision of the Cuban-United States commercial treaty to permit the island to trade with the entire world; moderate land reform; nationalization of key natural resources; and labor legislation. Other anti-Machadistas joined the ABC, a secret terrorist association of young professional men from the finest families. Organized in 1931 by a physician, Joaquín Martínez Sáenz, the ABC adopted the teachings of the Peruvian Raúl Haya de la Torre, founder of the Aprista movement. Its platform, slightly more conservative than that of the Directorio, also included abrogation of the Platt Amendment.

Even before the revolt of the students, intellectuals of the first republican-born generation had castigated the venality and laxity of their society. In 1923 Julio Antonio Mella, a student editor and writer, opened his campaign to purge the National University of old evils. In the famous Protesta de los Trece, thirteen of Havana's youthful intellectuals, in disapproval of one of the public scandals of the day, walked out of the Academy of Science during the appearance of President Zaya's Minister of Justice. Intellectual and political protest united in a common front after the poet Rubén Martínez Villena published his denunciation of the crimes of the Zaya regime.

The Grupo Minorista spoke for the new critics, intellectuals, professors, and students, who condemned the immortality around them. Nationalistic and sympathetic to reform, they demanded the purification of society and a return to the principles of Martí. The Minoristas represented a literary and artistic renaissance, as well as a political movement that sought to awaken the national conscience. José Ingenieros, the Argentine philosopher, provided the inspiration, while admiration and sympathy for the Soviet Union, the China of Sun Yat Sen, and the popular heroes of the Mexican Revolution contributed an element of militancy. The Minoristas defended national values and urged the solidarity of Spanish

America against "Yankee imperialism." Meanwhile, revisionist historians such as José Antonio Fernández de Castro and Emilio Roig de Leuchsenring reinterpreted the history of Cuba or wrote on socio-economic themes. Ramiro Guerra y Sánchez published his *Azucar y Población en las Antillas,* which recalled the critical studies of the master, José Antonio Saco.

The dissent of the twenties also created a social-protest literature in which the basic theme was a concern for the *guajiro* and worker. Agustín Acosta's melancholy poem, *La Zafra,* which depicted the life of the sugar workers, won national acclaim, as did stories of country life by Luis Felipe Rodríquez. As Negro and mulatto began to demand their place in society, there emerged the *negrista* movement, the intellectual and artistic voice of the Afro-Cuban. The spokesmen were Ramón Guirao, José Z. Tallet, and Nicolás Guillén, whose poems and stories expressed the Negro's hopes for the future and his despair of yesteryear.

Anti-Machado protest, in essence, had its origins in the history of Cuba. Each republican administration, in the opinion of the new critics, had contributed its quota of mistakes to the national problem. Every administration shared the blame for alienation of national resources, theft of public funds, political chicaneries, and the practice of calling on Americans to salvage personal interest. To the new critics, that process had merely culminated in Machado. The problem, in summary, was a society no longer acceptable to the young, the intelligentsia, and the nationalists.

Unable to provide a remedy for economic maladies, under attack by students, intellectuals, and labor, and eventually betrayed by his own army, Machado resigned on August 12, 1933. A public orgy greeted the news of his flight from Cuba. In their thirst for revenge, crazed mobs jammed the streets of Havana, looting, stealing, and killing *porristas* (Machado's thugs) and those cronies of the dictator who did not flee with him. Some were literally hacked to pieces in the public squares. In the meantime, those who had led the struggle against Machado demanded large-scale, nationalist, and often radical reforms. The slogan was "Cuba for the Cubans," a plea that had strong popular backing.

But the old political and military lords of Cuba elevated one of their own kind to the presidency, Carlos Manuel de Céspedes, upon whom the American ambassador in Havana had bestowed his blessings. A few days later, a revolt led by students from the National University and rank-and-file soldiers deposed the Céspedes regime, and appointed a junta of five under Ramón Grau San Martín, a professor from the University who, less than a week later (September 10, 1933), became provisional president of Cuba. He governed for one hundred and twenty eventful days and then fell from power, victim of an army plot hatched by a former sergeant, the machinations of politicians, the hostile diplomacy of the United States, and his own ineptness.

That brief interlude of one hundred and twenty days represents a watershed in the Republic's history: life on one side of it is not quite the same as life on the other. Although Grau and his disciples labored almost in vain, and their failure left fundamental questions unanswered, the revolution disrupted history—damaging but not transforming the national fabric. Cubans must shoulder the chief responsibility for their failure; the revolution simply succumbed to the evils of the local heritage. Yet American diplomacy was also directly accountable for the death of reform and the tragic aftermath.

[IV]

Older critics of Machado had simply wanted him ousted, believing that, with the restoration of public order and the constitution of 1901, the nation would return to normal. But the youthful rebels, insists Francisco Ichazo, had not deposed the tyrant merely to restore the past but to eliminate social and economic injustices as well as to correct political malpractices. Further, many revolutionaries resented strongly the powerful role that foreigners, Americans in particular but also Spaniards, played in Cuban affairs. Thus one of the goals of the revolutionaries was a greater degree of political and economic sovereignty for Cuba.

If those goals were blurred by the events surrounding the fall of Machado, in which the Directorio, the ABC, and alienated politicians united in common cause, they were manifest in the circumstances that produced the demise of the Céspedes regime. Students, professors, and reformers, their protests backed by the rifles of common soldiers, were responsible for the fall of Céspedes, who, in their opinion, did not speak for the revolution. In that allegation the revolutionaries had the facts on their side. Céspedes, son of the man who had fired the opening salvos of the Ten Years' War, was a conservative who had spent much of his life outside Cuba in the diplomatic service and hardly knew or understood the Cuban people. While Cuban Minister to France, he dedicated in eulogistic phrases a volume of his essays to Machado. Wealthy, scholarly, and impeccably honest, Céspedes resembled Tomás Estrada Palma, first President of the Republic, and, like his famous predecessor, he believed that Cuba's welfare was inextricably linked with the United States. But unlike Estrada Palma, Céspedes was indecisive, a man, to quote Enrique Lumen, with "the backbone of a lettuce leaf." Inaugurated President at 9:30 in the morning, he sought advice from the American Ambassador twice before that day ended. In place of the pro-American Céspedes, the students specifically demanded a national political convention, blueprints for socio-economic reform, and free and honest elections.

That job was entrusted to Ramón Grau San Martin, chief

of the Partido Revolucionario Cubano, the Auténticos, who were committed to making the "authentic" revolution—that promised by Martí. Grau was the son of a wealthy and distinguished family, a tall, thin, anemic-looking man, with a long, lantern-shaped face, who was a popular professor of physiology at the National University. A brilliant and successful physician, Grau had a large, private clientele in fashionable circles. For his underground opposition, during which he helped organize the Directorio Estudiantil Universitario, Machado had jailed Grau on the Isle of Pines. Then, after Grau saved the life of one of Machado's cronies on the operating table, the *caudillo* commuted his sentence on condition that he leave Cuba. In the course of his exile Grau spent two years in Florida. Critics charge that his student supporters had to plead with him to return to Cuba to assume command of the new regime.

The reforms enacted by the Grau administration opened a Pandora's box of political passions and rivalries that were not stilled until 1944—and then only temporarily. The revolutionary interlude proved short and Grau's place was taken by Carlos Mendieta, an army colonel and politician of the old school, who was, reported Ruby Hart Phillips of the New York *Times*, "highly conservative and amenable to advice from the American government," a man who had not "had a new idea in twenty years."

No single explanation provides a satisfactory answer for Grau's demise. As chief executive he proved weak, procrastinating on key decisions or leaving them to others, while his administrative ability was virtually nil. He was a neophyte in the world of practical politics; questions of ideology bored him—he claimed that his regime was "apolitical." He wanted, nonetheless, social justice for his people, but his romantic faith was not reciprocated by Cubans, who could not understand him. In Marxist terminology, Grau was more capitalist than revolutionary. Yet, as in the case of Franklin D. Roosevelt in the United States, the élite of Cuba, to which Grau belonged, saw him as a traitor to his class. In one respect, however, Grau marched in step with his youthful supporters: he was a militant nationalist; his slogan was "Cuba for the Cubans." He urged tight controls on foreign capital and backed laws to rid Cuban labor of foreigners, which gave his administration an undeserved radical tinge. Grau captured the presidency with the aid of students; once in office, however, they overwhelmed his administration and complicated the task of government, their idealism and enthusiasm proving poor substitutes for experience.

Grau, nevertheless, survived for more than four months. In that time his administration enacted far-reaching reforms. Despite the turmoil that hostile critics associate with his rule, order and stability were emerging—in the face of the hostility of the United States and the unemployment of the *tiempo muerto*. Grau's government committed costly blunders but, despite them, successfully overcame many of its original limitations and learned, in the process, to manage wisely the economic and political apparatus. Further, the Grau regime, which proved no less politically effective than many previous administrations, was winning popular support—in particular, to cite Charles A. Thomson, among the colored population (which encouraged racial conflict with anti-Grau whites). When Grau left for his exile abroad, vast throngs of saddened Cubans came to wish him well.

If this interpretation is correct, it is difficult not to conclude that American policy, as well as domestic difficulties, proved responsible for Grau's fall. He failed because he never received Washington's endorsement; nonrecognition by the State Department led to his undoing. As long as he lacked American recognition he could not organize a totally stable government. Yet, according to the State Department, Grau did not merit recognition until he had demonstrated his ability to impose total order and guarantee private property which, paradoxically, he could not do without recognition. Thus American policy encouraged the very condition it decried and kept alive the hopes of Grau's political enemies, encouraging them in their opposition to his government.

Ironically, the United States was not completely free to act independently in the crisis of 1933. In reality, the State Department was almost literally compelled to intervene by events in Cuba and the Cubans themselves. American involvement in the political crisis began in the final days of Machado's administration when hundreds of Cuban exiles, including some of the most distinguished *políticos*, established themselves in Florida and New York, where they waged an unrelenting propaganda campaign against the *caudillo*. Machado's political enemies in Cuba and the United States demanded in one form or another that the American government help them to unseat Machado; a minority even advocated direct intervention. On the island matters went from bad to worse as Machado employed terror to quell terror. As he ruthlessly attacked his enemies, his Cuban critics and the American press, swayed partly by sympathy for the rebels and partly by the pressure of American business interests concerned for their investments on the island, increased their demands for United States intervention.

This was the situation that confronted the recently elected Democratic administration. In the spring of 1933, according to Charles A. Thomson, Cuba represented Franklin D. Roosevelt's major challenge in the field of foreign affairs. No simple solution was available. Machado adamantly refused to resign, his opposition grew daily stronger and more vociferous, and chaos threatened American markets and interests on the island. New Deal economists, on the other hand, had envisaged recovery from the Great Depression partly in terms of increased exports to Latin America, with Cuba an especially lucrative possibility. Meanwhile, Latin American opinion had no stomach for further American intervention on the island.

The Cuban problem, therefore, had to be handled with care. To deal with the complex situation, Roosevelt named as ambassador to Cuba his old friend Sumner Welles, a seasoned diplomat and chief of the Latin American division of the State Department in the days of President Harding. Welles knew the Caribbean intimately, having served as a mediator in Santo Domingo, Honduras, and Nicaragua. He arrived in Havana early in May 1933 guided, according to Carlos Márquez Sterling, Cuban diplomat and politician, by the "preventive formula"—acceptance of a modified form of intervention to avoid outright intervention after the cause. By thus stealing a march on events, Washington hoped to prevent a crisis which would compel it to intervene in the old manner.

Welles required three months to find a way out of the morass. In the end, he adopted the one solution open to him: to ask Machado to resign. Peace was impossible until the tyrant departed, for Machado had lost all popular support. His control rested exclusively on the army and his political henchmen, who abandoned him after Welles announced that the United States would not accept him any longer. The activity of Welles unseated Machado, but the groundwork for his demise had been prepared before Welles's arrival on the island. After the general strike of August, which brought business to a standstill, Welles merely hastened the inevitable and, had he ended his mediation at this juncture, could have departed a hero. Unhappily for the future, Welles attempted to dictate a post-Machado settlement, which sank American policy in a political quicksand.

To defeat Grau, Welles had to rely on Fulgencio Batista, whose political career colors the history of Cuba until 1959. Just thirty-two years old, Batista symbolized a Cuban rags-to-riches story. In one sense, he was a man of the people, a Horatio Alger. Born in Oriente Province in 1901 of mixed racial parentage, he was the grandson of a Chinese peasant who had settled in Cuba in the nineteenth century and married a native Cuban, whose racial background probably included an African ancestor or two. "From his Chinese grandfather," writes Hudson Strode in his *Pageant of Cuba,* Batista "inherited his flat nose and his ability to disguise his designs behind a cryptic mask. . . ." Dark, uncomely, and short of stature, but with a body toughened by years of hardship, Batista learned to compensate for such handicaps with an agile mind. He joined the army in 1921, rose slowly but steadily through the ranks, and was promoted to sergeant-stenographer in 1928. Along the way he learned typing and shorthand, studied law, dealt in real estate, sold fruits and vegetables, managed a farm, taught commercial subjects in night school, and tutored the children of army officers. Later, in his post as boss of the army, he compensated for his lack of formal education by employing instructors to teach him and his wife the social graces. He read avidly, particularly studies of such men as the Italian dictator Benito Mussolini, whom he admired.

Charming, personable, and *simpático,* ever with a smile on his lips, Batista accommodated himself to the whims of his superiors, becoming the officers' "Man Friday," doing whatever was asked of him quickly and efficiently. Gregarious by nature and a persuasive talker, qualities that won him a large and enthusiastic following among the enlisted men, Batista possessed keen intuition and knew instinctively the proper move. As boss of Cuba, he wooed both labor and the conservatives. To win the favor of the latter, he visited the United States in 1938; then, to assure labor backing, flew to Mexico the next year and conferred with leftist President Lázaro Cárdenas, whom he dubbed "a leader of democracy." But Batista, as Ruby Hart Phillips remarked, was "too ambitious to have radical leanings." A realist first and always, he knew, as Strode perceptively recognized, that "diligence would not take him into the high ranks, or raise his pay from $60 a month to $600," for only the well-born won army commissions. The political troubles of 1933 offered Batista an opportunity to overcome this handicap.

Early in September 1933, after the officers at Camp Columbia had retired for the night, Batista and his fellow-conspirators occupied their posts and assumed command of the army. To support his coup, Batista had initially wooed the ABC, which he had joined in 1931, but when it rejected him, he turned to the faculty and students of the University and won their allegiance. In October, after the former army commanders barricaded themselves in the Hotel Nacional and defied the provisional government, Batista, now a colonel, personally led the attack on them. After a bloody battle that raged for nearly six hours, the officers surrendered, with seventeen dead and twenty-odd wounded.

Probably no one knows precisely what prompted Batista to betray his commanders and support Grau. Evidence indicates that he may have envisaged himself in the role of the paternalistic boss who heeded the cries of the discontented— which his acute political instincts told him it would be foolish to ignore. Batista's army and the university students kept Grau in office for four months. Then, convinced that Grau would not receive Washington's blessings, a point impressed upon him by Welles and his successor in Havana, Jefferson Caffery, Batista betrayed Grau and the revolution. Mendieta, the new conservative chieftain, enjoyed the backing of both Welles and Batista.

By relying on Batista and his army, Welles inadvertently introduced an old Latin American evil to Cuba. From that point on, every civilian regime lay at the mercy of the military, especially while Batista remained a factor in the island's political life, because Batista emerged from the Machado-Grau troubles as the new *caudillo* and the army as the arbiter of the nation's destiny.

Since Welles had meddled directly in the island's domestic

troubles, he had to choose between the two camps struggling for political supremacy. In his decision to back Céspedes and later Mendieta, which identified American interests with the conservatives, he alienated liberal Cubans. Even nationalist reformers had looked with favor on Welles's earlier efforts. To Felix Lizaso, intellectual and ally of university students, Welles merited praise for his activity in the Machado affair. "We could not have liberated ourselves of the hated regime," he assured his readers, "without the mediation of the United States, [which was] not intervention, but the act of a good neighbor." Only the Directorio Universitario, Machado's cronies, and Communist labor leaders had opposed Welles's mediation. But his subsequent intrigues shattered that idyllic picture. Conservatives remained friendly, but nationalists and revolutionaries turned hostile. In their eyes, Welles had trampled on the revolution, frustrating its promise to rid Cuba of its foreign yoke. Herminio Portell-Vilá, then a youthful intellectual, labeled Welles's efforts a "hypocritical form of intervention . . . proof that the Good Neighbor . . . meant and still means . . . the ruin of Cuba." Thus, Welles's policies fed anti-American feeling and eventually harmed American interests.

Why, then, did the astute Wells adopt a policy which, from historical hindsight, was of dubious merit? One can only speculate, but one conclusion seems unavoidable: though he had spent embattled years in the diplomatic service in Latin America, the Ambassador had no empathy with the revolution. A cold, phlegmatic man who, according to a commonly held view on the island, judged Cubans with an air of superiority, Welles had nothing in common with the bold, brash, and youthful rebels. He was "an impeccable and enigmatic diplomat," recalled Enrique Lumen, who knew "how to tie his cravat correctly and to wear his jacket in the bluestocking manner, with a flower in his lapel and his shoes always polished, [but] obtuse in his thinking and shortsighted in his vision." As his diplomatic negotiations with Mexico later demonstrated, Welles was a conservative who worshipped law and order, abhorred revolution, and believed private property sacrosanct. His instincts invariably led him to side with American interests, for he had matured during the nonrevolutionary period of Latin American history, in which American policy-makers had the final say. By background and training, Welles was unprepared to cope with a Cuba in the midst of change. Confronted with the explosive situation on the island, he fell back on past experience, which told him to squash the surface trouble and proceed as though nothing had occurred.

Temperament and political differences do not tell the entire story, however, for Welles formulated his own interpretation of Cuba's woes. In his opinion, economics, not political and moral issues, had sired the island's troubles. The problem was to restore prosperity, as well as to eliminate the glaring evils of the dictatorship, upon which the unemployed vented their frustrations. Once the economy was sound again, which meant revival of the sugar industry, political questions would take care of themselves. Prosperity would put an end to political discontent and benefit everyone. Cubans would have jobs, food, and political stability; in turn, they would buy American goods, which would nourish the lagging economy of the United States. In the process, the danger to American interests on the island would disappear.

Frightened by the specter of a revolutionary rabble wielding political power, in particular the growing enthusiasm of the colored population for the reforms of the Grau regime, and distrustful of the ability of an inexperienced administration to control its more militant backers, moderate middle-sector Cubans who accepted the need for political reform but not basic economic change ultimately endorsed Welles's formula. Its success led to the downfall of the Grau regime, which the Ambassador labeled radical and even Communist, and to the restoration of the old order. Only Machado's closest collaborators were shorn of their authority.

Welles's economic hypothesis, which linked American and Cuban welfare, explains his antipathy to the revolutionary government. Unless their declarations were dismissed as meaningless, the rebels had in mind reforms that would substantially modify the local economy and the character of American interests in Cuba. The crux of the revolution of 1933, Francisco Ichazo stated, was an exalted economic nationalism directed primarily at foreign holdings. The goals of revolution were the betterment of the workers' lot, land reform, and an end to racial discrimination, which was identified with the exploitation of Afro-Cubans by vested interests. The rebels envisaged a national moral regeneration that would cleanse the body politic of impurities, cast out the *caudillos* and their political parties, end the greedy scurryings after power, and open public life to the generation deprived of a voice in government by the Zayas and Machados.

The revolutionaries acted rapidly to heed local pleas for reform. Their decrees established the eight-hour day, fixed minimum wage levels, and created a Ministry of Labor with authority to enforce compulsory arbitration of industrial disputes. Other reforms gave the workers control of their unions and excluded foreigners from labor posts. A milestone was passed in the Nationalization of Labor Law, which stipulated that no less than half the work force of any given industry be composed of native Cubans and banned the practice of importing cheap labor from the Antilles. Later, the government organized a Colono Association of small planters and granted a quota to the small mills. There were blueprints for agrarian legislation, including procedures for the purchase of the bankrupt Cuba Cane Company. The National University of Havana was granted autonomy.

In enacting its reforms, the revolutionary government became embroiled in quarrels with three foreign-owned corporate giants. After labor difficulties shut down the plants, the government seized the Delicias and Chaparra properties of the Cuban-American Sugar Company. Convinced that the Chase National Bank had supported Machado, the government cancelled payment on an 80 million dollar loan from the Bank. Clashes with the Cuban Electric Company over rates in Havana led the government to operate the company's plant.

American interests more than three decades old, controlling nearly two-thirds of the sugar output, were at stake. Many of the mills were owned by refineries, holding companies, and banks in the United States; the National City Bank, to cite a specific case, owned nine mills. Virtually all banking was done by American and Canadian institutions; the two leading firms were the Royal Bank of Canada and the Chase National Bank. United States currency was the legal tender. (Cuba did not have a national bank of issue until 1948.) The Cuban Telephone Company, a subsidiary of International Telephone and Telegraph, provided telephone service; another American corporation held a monopoly on light and power; the railroads were British- and American-owned. The economic masters of Cuba, in short, were foreigners.

United States businessmen with investments in Cuba refused to accept the revolutionary regime and asked Washington to intercede in their behalf. The State Department, which undoubtedly sympathized with them, required no prodding, the New Deal administration having wrought no fundamental change in foreign policy. As Bryce Wood says, Roosevelt's administration considered economic and diplomatic pressure, the threat of "intervention," and "free" advice as justifiable elements of Cuban policy. The issue, moreover, was not just Cuba but Latin America, where nationalists, spurred on by the Great Depression, were beginning to urge limits to the rights of foreigners and expropriation of their properties. Exports to Cuba, which had fallen off since passage of the Hawley-Smoot Tariff Act, were another problem.

Welles's policy must be evaluated in the light of concern for export markets and safeguards for American property abroad. The objective was to stabilize the local situation, which Welles interpreted essentially in economic terms. In his judgment, American "commercial and export interests in Cuba" could not be revived by the provisional government, and Welles therefore aligned himself with the conservatives whose economic and political interests linked them closely to the United States. With the revolutionaries out of the picture, Welles and his colleagues in Washington moved to buttress the Mendieta-Batista regime.

After Grau fell, Washington abrogated the Platt Amendment. From the moment of his arrival in Havana, Welles had made no secret of the fact that when Cuba had a "stable regime" his government was ready to cancel the Platt Amendment and provide economic assistance. Washington was playing a double game, offering concessions in return for a change of administration or, at least, modification of policy. This double-edged diplomacy undermined the revolutionary government. Cuban politicians of the old school, who had no stomach for reform, could offer the people a political victory and economic concessions in exchange for the demise of Grau. Cubans could have the Platt Amendment relegated to limbo if they permitted Washington and the conservatives to depose the revolutionaries.

Nevertheless, that concession, whether born of opportunism or not, conceded the Cubans a tangible conquest. Although Washington kept Guantánamo, the Republic was free of outright tutelage for the first time in history. To the nationalists, writes Félix Lizaso, abrogation of the Platt Amendment marked a milestone, while for the professional politicians its abrogation and the economic concessions later granted by the United States helped to silence popular clamor for change. Small wonder, then, that the conservative Manuel Márquez Sterling, whose untiring diplomatic efforts had assured the diplomatic triumph, could remark that with the demise of the Platt Amendment he could "die in peace."

American economic aid arrived in two packages. The Jones-Costigan Act of May 1934, which assigned sugar quotas to foreign producers, granted Cuba approximately 28 per cent of the American market and, in addition, the Reciprocity Act of August 1934 lowered tariffs on raw Cuban sugar and offered preferential treatment to thirty-five products from the island. In appreciation, nearly 300,000 Cubans signed a letter of gratitude addressed to President Roosevelt. The Cuban government, however, had to give in return preferential treatment to 400 American items—which severely limited possibilities of its industrial development.

The prescriptions helped mend the health of the Mendieta-Batista regime; quotas and lower duties revived sugar exports. The United States also profited, as Cuban imports from the United States rose nearly 60 per cent in 1934–35. Outwardly, all ended well: the unpredictable Grau was safely out of the way, radical reforms were postponed, American property was safe, sugar barons were back in the saddle, and more people had jobs and money. Cuba had returned to normal.

6.

The Old Order Returns

*The problem of the latifundium is by no means
solved in Cuba. With the treaty, the United States
has temporarily alleviated the Cuban crisis and has
saved from total ruin for the moment most of
the North American capital invested in the Cuban
sugar business. . . . But actually the latifundium
problem remains unchanged and Cuba, now
economically more dependent than ever on the
fluctuations of the United States trade policy, is less
free to expand its trade with the rest of the world.*
RAMIRO GUERRA Y SANCHEZ

*The last three years of Batista's regime were in
large part a repetition of the last years of Machado.*
SPECIAL WARFARE AREA HANDBOOK
FOR CUBA

[I]

But Cuban reformers lost their revolution.

Not only were popular aspirations thwarted by the events
of 1933, but Washington's concessions, which rescued the

island from the doldrums, left chronic ills intact. King sugar emerged from the crisis a strengthened lord of Cuba, while nothing was done to modify the monocultural nature of the economy. Due to the troubles of the twenties and the low prices that prevailed until 1934, the giant mills alone survived, nearly all backed by American capital. The smaller units went bankrupt. After 1933, fewer mills operated, and because of the relatively smaller size of the quota (compared to pre-1934) granted Cuban sugar in the American market, the mills were unable to operate at full capacity. Thus, the length of the *zafra* was cut in half, which meant many fewer jobs than in the prosperous days of yesteryear.

Recovery was a reality, but its pace proved slow, and according to the terms of the quota system, the size of the quota would never permit the Cuban sugar industry to return to predepression levels of production. With a glutted world market, moreover, which each year took a thinner slice of Cuba's total production, the islanders were compelled to depend on their share of the American market. The quota system, therefore, stabilized the economy at low levels of production and work. Julio J. Le Riverend Brusone, a Cuban economist, complained that the quota system would account for less than half the potential sugar production of Cuba. "The Sugar Act of 1934 and the reciprocal trade agreement," according to Philip W. Bonsal, "raised the island from the desperate straits caused by the depression plus our tariff to a level of genteel poverty with sugar income only 50 per cent below the average for the twenties instead of the 75 per cent of the disaster years [1932 and 1933]." Thus, as long as Cuba remained essentially a sugar exporter, it could not expand production, having no market for its exportable surplus. To complicate matters, the quota act guaranteed no fixed or permanent share of the American market but left determination of the annual quota on a contractual basis dependent on the whims of Congress. After

1934 a number of cuts in the Cuban quota were made for the benefit of American domestic producers and even, adds Bonsal, of foreign producers. "The need for Cuba to avoid actions or attitudes which might put her in a bad light with Congress at quota time," the former Ambassador concedes, "was a fact of life generally understood."

Until vigorous efforts were made to transform the economy, which the failure of the revolution postponed or cancelled, production would lag behind previous levels. To cite the Foreign Policy Association analysis of 1935, *Problems of the New Cuba,* the island had to develop non-sugar crops, above all small sustenance farms to support the rural population in the *tiempo muerto* and, eventually, an agricultural middle class. If Cuba failed to rebuild its economy, the Association experts warned, the commercial treaty would keep alive political and economic evils. Unfortunately for subsequent Cuban-American relations, a temporary improvement in both the price and size of the export market for sugar during World War II kept Cuban leaders from heeding the advice of the experts. Of the island's exportable product in 1958, sugar accounted for approximately four-fifths of Cuban sales abroad.

No efforts, furthermore, were made to disturb the island's almost complete reliance on industrialized nations. The Cuban economy remained a victim of each international business cycle. More than ever before, the island was intimately wedded to the economy of its powerful neighbor. In addition, as Wyatt MacGaffey and Clifford R. Barnett stress, the Cubans eventually developed a trade deficit with the United States. By 1959 Cuban exports to the United States, which had constituted 80 per cent of the island's total exports between 1902 and 1945, had declined to 69 per cent. However, imports of American goods, 66 per cent of the island's total imports in the era from 1911 to 1940, had risen to 75 per cent by 1956. In summary, Cuba was less autonomous economically than previously. In order to sell sugar in the American market, it had to promise to purchase almost exclusively from the United States. Cuba's welfare, complained Herminio Portell-Vilá, was in American hands. Any United States decision to suspend or lower the quota, or to raise the duty on Cuban sugar, would send "a chill into the heart of every Cuban," for a smaller quota or a lower price meant a shrinkage of national income, increased unemployment, fewer working days, a drop in purchases abroad, and a subsequent decline in customs duties, which supplied half the government's revenue.

The settlement of 1934, in a capsule, left intact the lopsided economy. One of the highest export rates in the world, but dependent totally on imports, including food; a high per capita income for Latin America, in an economy burdened by seasonal and chronic unemployment; a sugar industry that kept the country alive, but survived on American markets and capital; a latifundia in the colonial mold, but heavily mechanized—these were the paradoxes of Cuba.

Cuban economists found the absence of new growth especially disheartening. No fundamental change in productive capacity had occurred since 1925. The base of the economy had been laid in the twenties. Until then, the rate of economic development had exceeded population growth, but in only five of the seven years from 1948 to 1954 had the gross national product grown at the 1947 rate; in only two, the wartime years of 1951 and 1952, had the growth of the GNP permitted an annual increase in the standard of living. If by 1965 Cubans were to enjoy a standard of living comparable to that of 1947, the island had to produce nearly 10 million tons of sugar, almost four million above the previous record. To permit a yearly 2 per cent rise in living standards, Cuba had to produce 14,763,000 tons. But to cite the 1950 report of the World Bank, stagnation had replaced dynamic development on the Cuban economic scene.

World War II revived the economy and created a bonanza that endured until the late forties. Of the leading sugar exporters, Cuba alone escaped the holocaust of war. The Korean War and the Suez Crisis, which checked recessionary drifts, provided new booms for the economy. On the negative side, the three crises sparked inflationary spirals that wiped out much of the gains; with few goods to buy and a flood of currency in circulation, the Cubans simply spent more, especially on luxury goods. In the cities, the cost of living climbed beyond the reach of wages, a trend that went unchecked throughout the fifties; in the countryside, prosperity never trickled down to rural workers. In 1958, moreover, approximately 25 per cent of the work force had jobs for only eight to nine months of the year, while about 9 per cent was unemployed the year round.

During and after World War II, the government of Cuba cast off all restraints on the size of the sugar crop. World War II and the Korean conflict made possible the sale of bumper crops but, once peace descended on the world again, Cuba faced its chronic overproduction problem. Thus, in 1952, the size of the sugar crop was once more curtailed, a policy made imperative by the existence of sugar surpluses at home and abroad. Throughout the fifties, production hovered at the five million ton mark, a figure impressive in itself but, in light of the growing population (from approximately 3.5 million in 1925 to 6.5 million in 1958), hardly large enough to provide prosperity for all the people.

The quota and reciprocity pacts, in addition, focused Cuban ire on the United States. The agreements benefited both countries; yet, by underwriting the sugar industry, they buttressed the American stake in it, making change difficult without antagonizing the United States. The American treasury, refineries, and shipping companies, meanwhile, had discovered a lucrative source of income in the duties and profits from the island's exports, which Cubans felt was at their expense. American businessmen had also captured the Cuban domestic market, replacing rivals who had previously supplied it. In the case of rice, Asian exporters were all but eliminated. Cuba purchased American dairy products, eggs, canned fruits, potatoes, vegetables, fish, poultry, and pork, and even became a net importer of alcoholic beverages. These goods, and a long list of manufactured articles, were purchased from the United States at prices higher than those at which Europe and Japan could have provided them. An almost identical situation had existed before 1934, but the 1933 revolution was waged to correct it.

Not merely the facts themselves, but what people think of them, is often the key to international relations. On the question of trade, Cubans believed that in the pacts of 1934, and their later revised versions, they had been victimized.

[II]

Even prior to the 1933 crisis, attempts to cope with economic maladies had irreversibly drawn Cuba into the vortex of twentieth-century state planning. Beginning in 1925, the year that saw the terrible economic crisis dawn, the government had undertaken to intervene directly in affairs previously left to private business. Machado's accomplishments in this respect were impressive, a point almost always overlooked by his critics. To provide employment, he had initiated a vast public works program. His tariff policy had explored ways to control imports and to encourage the growth of native industry. Unhappily for Cuba, the economic decline and his own graft-ridden and corrupt administration had sabotaged much of the effort.

The revolution, and the repercussions of the American quota-price system which imposed on Cuba a greater need for national self-discipline, added new impetus to the movement in behalf of state planning. One result was to make the state more concerned with popular welfare. (Castro inherited this legacy; he did not pioneer an entirely new role for the state in economic planning.) That preoccupation was manifest in Grau's legislation, in the failure to rescind the bulk of it after his departure from office, and in the national charter of 1940. Labor, especially, received additional benefits—often at the expense of the large sugar corporations: for example, the law of 1937 protected the interest of *colonos* and established wage-scales for cane-cutters. Despite its weaknesses, the character of the new legislation was progressive; it was, however, only half-way reform, which neither answered national needs nor quieted popular discontent.

This ambiguity was embodied in the Constitution of 1940. Offspring of the frustrations of the thirties, of a revolution which had failed to eliminate their cause, the charter was a potpourri of liberal remedies. It was conceived as a response to the recession of the late thirties, but at a time when the reform spirit was on the wane and the uncertainty, anguish, and abnormality of the decade were disappearing. Francisco Ichazo was on firm ground when he noted that the Constitution was one of the progressive documents of the era; however, instead of legislating the revolution into existence, it marked its culmination.

The Constitution was more progressive in general philosophy than on specific issues. With respect to the state's authority over private property, it was more protective than its predecessor. It called for indemnification in cash for private property expropriated by the government—which the constitution of 1901, a timid document on economic matters, had not. Gustavo Gutiérrez, one of the framers of the 1940 Constitution, blamed influential interests for this restrictive "contraband" clause. As a charter, the Constitution reflected the passions and divided loyalties of its sponsors. Since the revolution of 1933, reformers had advocated constitutional revision but urged that its architects be chosen by popular vote independent of party affiliations, on the assumption that the parties did not speak for the national will. "First the constitution and then elections" had been the slogan. Despite demands that popular sentiments be heeded, however, the parties had controlled the political apparatus and thus the election of delegates. Of the 81 delegates, the Socialist-Democratic coalition, speaking for the Batista-backed administration, elected 36, including four Communists; the Opposition block elected 45, with 18 from the Partido Revolucionario Cubano and 17 from the standpat Partido Democrático Republicano. Apparently the Auténtico-led block controlled the convention, but in reality formed a minority. Eventually, the Partido Democrático Republicano switched sides, giving the Batista coalition the king-making role. Of the 286 articles in the Constitution, 236 had been approved under the leadership of the Batista coalition.

Despite the failure of the reformers to control the convention, the delegates wrote a forward-looking charter. The explanation lies in a number of factors. In 1940 popular opinion undoubtedly still mirrored the aspirations of the revolution which the recession years of the late thirties had kept alive. After all, Cubans never truly recovered from the consequences of the twenties until World War II revived their economy. The thirties were years of experimentation, of the corporate states of Germany and Italy, the New Deal, and, perhaps more meaningful for Cuba, Lázaro Cárdenas' leftist regime in Mexico and the fascist-leaning Estado Novo of Getulio Vargas in Brazil. Local thinking reflected these currents.

Critics of the status quo had also discovered an unexpected ally in Batista. Though his army formed a bulwark of the conservative regimes, Batista often proved a reformer in practice. To alleviate the lot of the poor, he had heeded labor demands, built rural schools, employed his soldiers to teach in them, and levied a tax on sugar to finance the program. When his conservative puppet, President Miguel Mariano Gómez, objected, Batista removed him from office. In 1937 Batista proposed a Three Year Plan which advocated controls for the sugar and tobacco industries, redistribution of the land, compulsory arbitration of labor disputes, and welfare measures. With presidential ambitions in mind for 1940, Batista walked a political tightrope—on the one hand supporting reformers in their call for a constitutional convention and, on the other, conservative demands for the election of delegates on a party basis.

The Constitution of 1940 was the product of this jumbled picture. It was supremely nationalistic; the goal was the *Cubanización de Cuba*. At the same time, in the Cuban tradition, it embodied a number of North American influences, including a system of city managers. The charter was strongly economic in character and laid special emphasis on the quest for social justice.

An examination of its articles reveals the extent of its commitment to progressive principles. Article 24 justified expropriation of property "for reason of public utility or social interest." Article 66 authorized the state to "employ all resources in its power to provide jobs for everyone." In Article 88, the charter claimed the subsoil for the state: "Land, forests, and concessions for the exploitation of the subsoil . . . and every other enterprise of public interest, must be exploited in a manner favorable to the social welfare." Article 90 banned latifundia and stipulated the "maximum amount of property that each person or corporation may possess for each type of exploitation . . . [and] acquisitions and possession of land by foreign persons and companies," and asked the state to "adopt measures tending to revert the land to Cuban ownership." Article 271 empowered the government to "direct the course of the national economy for the benefit of the people . . . to promote national agriculture and industry, facilitating their diversification as sources of public wealth and collective benefit." Article 272 subjected foreign ownership and the use of property to national laws. Article 275 authorized state control of the sugar industry. The Constitution also had provisions spelling out labor benefits: the right to a job, an eight-hour day, minimum wages, compulsory union membership, collective bargaining, vacations with pay, accident and sickness insurance, and old-age pensions. Only a profound revolution would make these provisions operative, while their enforcement would limit dramatically American control of the local economy. Further, these provisions explain why Fidel Castro, and other reformers who advocated fundamental changes in the Cuban economy, would eventually demand the restoration and enforcement of the Constitution of 1940.

Unfortunately, the rulers of Cuba were permitted to interpret the charter loosely, for the framers of the Constitution left its implementation largely to the Cuban congress, which was to pass *leyes complementarias* to enforce the provisions in the document. The Constitution was largely meaningless, as Gutiérrez pointed out, unless congress acted; and the congress, though it passed a number of important measures, never enforced the bulk of the document, partly because World War II revived the economy, shelving the national plea for reform, and partly because the politicians who dictated policy ignored their obligations. Also, the courts and the executive were generally unsympathetic.

The framers of the document erred in another manner. In their desire to curtail Batista, whom reformers and conservatives both distrusted, they established a "parliamentary" system, including a prime minister and council, theoretically responsible to congress. But in their haste to shear executive authority, the lawmakers forgot to reckon with the hard facts of Cuban political life. In juxtaposition, they called for congressional supremacy, but left the prime minister at the mercy of an executive who possessed the power to declare a "state of emergency." Congress had to give its approval but, since the president controlled the legislature, either directly or through his party, he possessed dictatorial powers. Thus the framers of the charter abandoned Cuba to the whims of a strongman.

Though the charter remained largely inoperative, as a blueprint for reform it was a legislative fact. Its promises, in addition, acted as a spur. Once the war prosperity disappeared, the Constitution would serve to remind Cubans of what remained unfinished and to reveal the contradictions between theory and reality. Attempts to unite theory and reality underlay much of the political turmoil of the fifties.

[III]

The crisis of 1933 and its dénouement promoted progressive legislation but had scant impact on politics. Cuba rapidly returned to its time-honored habits and, like a worn and broken record, the scratchy tune of Cuban politics was heard again.

In 1934 three political groups were left to battle for

control of the island's ruling apparatus. Batista and his cronies and the professional politicians formed two camps, which usually united in common cause. Arrayed against them were the Auténticos, who probably spoke for a majority of the population. It was a struggle between the Auténticos, the self-proclaimed heirs of Martí who wanted to revise the constitution and proceed with reform and their opposition, which clung to the status quo or at least to postponement of legislative reform until a more favorable time. Little was accomplished because Grau and his cohorts stood aloof from elections which, they charged, were rigged by their enemies.

The conservatives, as a result, preempted the country's political structure, which Batista—who emerged the national *caudillo* partly because the Auténticos permitted him to depict himself as the people's protector—manipulated from behind the scenes. Batista captured the questionable allegiance of the practical politicians because they preferred him to the Auténticos, and he quickly demonstrated that his recently acquired allies had not misplaced their faith in him. He kept the cauldron from boiling over, beginning with his brutal repression of the general strike of 1935, which almost proved fatal to Carlos Mendieta.

Prodded by Batista, the venerable politicians buried the hatchet. In the Pacta Institucional Rivero-Zayas, they consented to restore the Constitution of 1901, after modifications were enacted, and to hold general elections in the fall of 1936. The economic difficulties of the late thirties and the increasingly non-revolutionary hue of the Auténticos prescribed additional conciliation. In 1939 Federico Laredo Bru, latest of Batista's puppet presidents, enticed his master and Ramón Grau San Martín into a conference where the two protagonists agreed to hold elections for a constitutional convention along party lines, thus ending the abstention from formal politics of the Auténticos. In the forties and fifties the scene took on a slightly different cast, though nothing basic changed despite the Constitution of 1940. Batista ruled from 1940 to 1944, and from 1952 until forced to flee in January 1959. In the interval, two Auténticos were in office, Grau San Martín, finally given his opportunity to run Cuba, and his protégé, Carlos Prío Socarrás.

Few of the revolutionary decrees were repealed, but little more than lip service was paid them. Under the provisional constitution of 1934 which had specifically safeguarded private property, the Havana plant of the Cuban Electric Company, which the revolutionary administration had seized, was returned to its owners. When, in desperation, embittered revolutionaries had resorted to violence, the Mendieta regime had suspended constitutional guarantees, declared a state of emergency, imposed the death penalty on terrorists, and promised severe punishment for persons who provoked political disorders, celebrated unauthorized political gatherings, or defied public officials. Special tribunals were organized to deal with offenders. To guarantee the *zafra*, the government had prohibited strikes, authorized the dissolution of labor unions that broke the law, and employed the army to arrest recalcitrant labor leaders.

Politics quickly recovered their customary ways. In the election of 1936 Miguel Mariano Gómez, a member of the ruling clans, emerged the victor, while in congress two factions split the seats between them. One, a coalition of Acción Republicana and the Unión Nacionalista, had captured the Senate from the Conjunto Nacional Democrático, but to avoid conflict, the Acción-Unión coalition had magnanimously permitted the Conjuncto Nacional seats in the Senate, from which the election returns had barred it. Gómez, however, had not mastered the congressional technique of compromise; he foolishly opposed Batista's cherished school project and found himself out of office. His place was taken by Vice President Laredo Bru, who saw the wisdom of the *caudillo's* schools.

Given the nature of local politics and the apathy of the *guajiro*, Batista, the candidate of an alliance of seven political parties, probably won the election of 1940 with no more fraud than usual. He had skilfully cultivated his path to the presidency—keeping the army loyal to him, rewarding labor unions and their leaders, and offering offices and spoils to bureaucrats and politicians. Businessmen and professionals, more concerned with stability and order than with reform, gave him unexpected support at the polls. Batista proved an able ruler, though he governed in the accepted tradition, enriching himself and his cronies. In 1944 he stepped down and permitted the election of his old rival, Grau San Martín, apparently convinced that he had mastered the local situation and that the middle-aged revolutionary generation had dissipated its fervor.

Events testify that Batista judged wisely. Grau, Prío, and their Auténticos proved inept and harmless. The weaknesses that Sumner Welles had perceived in Grau were soon transparent. Embittered by the treatment accorded him by his ancient foes, Grau watched passively as the hungry Auténticos turned on Batista's henchmen, whose boss had retired to Florida to spend his wealth on a second wife, daughter of a prominent family.

The old political wars between the Auténticos and their rivals broke out almost immediately. But now only public office and pecuniary gain were at stake, for the Auténticos had succumbed to the vices they had censured as youthful rebels. Wartime prosperity presented unlimited opportunity for graft and corruption which, lamented Francisco Ichazo, suborned politicians and public alike. Prío Socarrás, Grau's successor, especially yielded to the temptation of easy money. By 1952, when Batista drove him into exile, Prío epitomized the Cuban politician's proclivity for the good and luxurious life. He had had a long and distinguished revolutionary record; his betrayal of past principles was thus all the more tragic.

In his student days, Prío had been a university radical and Secretary-General of the Havana Directorio Estudiantil which opened the anti-Machado struggle and, because of his activities, had spent nearly three years in prison. He had presided over the revolutionary junta at Camp Columbia the night Batista had taken command of the military, was a founder of the Auténtico Party, and had subsequently participated in the drafting of the 1940 constitution. In 1947 Grau had appointed him Secretary of Labor. Prío received his presidential sash at a critical juncture, for the end of World War II, which revived the old problem of local over-production, and the appearance of new sugar producers on the world market threatened Cuba's prosperity. In October 1948 his administration faced a financial crisis brought on by declining revenues, which the Grau regime squandered on grandiose public works and graft. Batista, elected senator in absentia in the elections of 1948, had meanwhile returned home. When he deposed the graft-ridden Prío administration in 1952, public protest was feeble.

The Batista of 1952 no longer spoke as the ambivalent politician who accepted the rules of Cuban politics but granted concessions to labor, built schools, and kept the party hacks in check. The restored dictator stepped out of the Machado mold. To quote the *Special Warfare Area Handbook for Cuba*, prepared by specialists at the American University: "The last three years of Batista's regime were in large part a repetition of the last years of Machado." The creaky party system, including the semi-independent labor force of the thirties, had virtually collapsed in the rubble of corruption and cynicism; the old alignments, which once had checked the proclivities of the dictator, had broken down. The public had accepted the state of affairs until the bonanza of the Korean War ended, but with the return of normal times, public unrest appeared again. Batista capitalized on it.

Batista aggravated rather than cured the malady. He postponed the elections scheduled for 1954, and then perpetrated an election farce in 1958. To hold on to power, he kept in step with Washington's anti-Communism, broke relations with the Soviet Union, drove native Communists underground, and signed a mutual assistance pact with Washington. This kept him in office, won over conservatives, and pleased the American State Department, but also cost him whatever sympathy and backing he may have had among nationalists and the young. When they protested, Batista resorted to terror.

[IV]

By 1958 Cuba had reached the end of another historical cycle. The first, dating back to 1902, had disappeared amidst the debris of the Machado dictatorship, the Great Depression, and the rise of the Republican-born generation of the twenties. The second, which emerged with the revolution of 1933, now closed. Despite the tangible gains of the thirties, the old evils still plagued the island. Of course, change had modified Cuba, and often in a profound sense; labor, the political factions, and the students were better organized than before, while the social and institutional pattern had suffered major alterations. But, in the minds of many Cubans, especially the young and impatient, this change was too slow or in the wrong direction. A case in point was the Grau regime of the forties which, in the opinion of some outside observers and of Cubans who had known the political scene of the twenties and thirties, had provided the best combination of relative freedom and order Cuba had ever experienced. To the young critics, however, the traditional corruption and political chicanery that characterized the regime more than overshadowed its positive attributes. Further, nothing was done to disturb the old reliance on sugar and the United States. The administration of Prío Socarrás not only antagonized the young, but alienated many who had supported Grau's regime. The effort to transform Cuba, in short, had failed, victim of the local heritage, weak leadership, and the refusal of the United States to accept the first Grau administration and its reforms. It was time, declared an increasingly frustrated generation, for another revolution.

That unrest found a spokesman in Eddie Chibás. His father, a wealthy Cuban, had been Secretary of Public Works in the Céspedes cabinet, which rumor claimed that Sumner Welles had hand-picked. In 1933, as a member of the Directorio Estudiantil, Chibás had joined other students in the coup that toppled Céspedes. Eventually he had entered the ranks of the Auténticos, supporting Grau for the presidency in 1944 and winning a senate seat for himself. In 1947 he founded the Partido del Pueblo Cubano, the Ortodoxos, who claimed to speak for the ideals of Martí, which they charged the Auténticos had cast aside in their rush to acquire wealth and power. Ultimately, Auténticos and Ortodoxos became mortal enemies. In preparation for the election of 1952, Chibás ran for the presidency in 1948 and made a good showing. He voiced the hopes of the intelligentsia and youth of the island, thoroughly disillusioned with the Auténticos. His crusade enshrined moral reform, demanding "honor before money."

Left-leaning Ortodoxos, however, asked for more than

spiritual bliss. In their opinion, only a complete housecleaning would bring relief. Such a program, they stressed, must espouse economic and social questions. "Political liberty," to quote an Ortodoxo slogan borrowed from Martí, "is possible only when it is accompanied by economic independence." Ortodoxos of this school demanded an end to the system that subjected Cuban freedom to the whims of foreigners and urged the diversification of the economy, disappearance of the latifundia, redistribution of idle lands, benefits for the *guajiro,* and equality for the Negro. Their program expressed Martí's romantic faith in the man who labored with his hands. In foreign affairs, these Ortodoxos denounced dictatorships in Latin America and insisted on the right of national self-determination. They viewed the Monroe Doctrine with a wary eye, condemned Yankee intervention in the Americas, advocated multilateral diplomacy, and pledged full cooperation with the United Nations but not with the OAS, while condemning Communism and declaring that people must choose between Communism and freedom. Among the disciples of this creed was Fidel Castro, then a youthful university student.

Chibás did not live to see the ultimate fruits of his protest. Apparently discouraged by the lack of sufficient public response to his pleas—or perhaps in an attempt to dramatize his protest—he committed suicide in August 1951. But he had ignited the flames of rebellion among the young. Before long, radical students, intellectuals, and discontented professionals had revived terror to combat Batista. In 1953 Castro and his band of young rebels, claiming Martí as their intellectual mentor, attacked the army garrison in Santiago, capital of Oriente, and in 1956 the leaders of the abortive uprising began their successful campaign to dethrone the *caudillo.* A year later, university students attempted to assassinate Batista. In the interim, they had revived the Directorio Estudiantil to combat the tyranny. A restless

population watched the proceedings with growing appre-
hension.

[V]

History, according to the cliché, never repeats itself. However, a survey of the events that produced Batista's final
downfall makes it difficult not to conclude that Cuban history, if it does not duplicate itself, occurs in cycles. An
apocryphal Republic, venal dictatorship, economic unrest,
and militant rebels prepared the stage. Responsibility for
the crisis lay primarily with the Cubans; but Sumner Welles,
the policy-makers who succeeded him, and American business interests were hardly blameless.

7.

The Strand of Socialism

Marxist theory which explains all social evolution in terms of economic factors is but the truth in exaggerated form. Economic necessities and the activities which they put into play are not the only prime movers of the complex social phenomena of a society; but they are responsible for the most obvious and decisive aspects of those phenomena.

ENRIQUE JOSE VARONA

[I]

Castro's embrace of Marxism-Leninism surprised his defenders in the United States and the majority of his supporters in Cuba. Both found themselves unable to explain their chieftain's conversion to Communism, while his enemies charged that he had deliberately betrayed the Revolution or kept secret his Communist background when fighting Batista. Yet Castro's Communism neither pioneered a new political stance nor broke with Cuban political tradition, for the record of socialism represents a major strand in the island's history.

Three fundamental necessities forced Castro into the Communist camp. First, his distrust and fear of American foreign policy which, he believed, opposed his goal of social revolution. Second, his need to rally and organize popular support behind his Revolution—especially that of organized labor. And third, his belief that Communism provided the answer to Cuba's socio-economic problems.

The Soviet Union furnished Castro with an opportunity to escape American hegemony in the Western Hemisphere. But the history of Cuba, and not merely the appeal of Marxist doctrines, explains Castro's shift from humanist reformer to Communist. For Cuban Communists not only built and controlled the first nation-wide labor organization in Cuba, but converted their political party—the most successful in Latin America—into a tightly knit unit that enjoyed wide popular support at the polls. The Cuban Communist movement, therefore, offered Castro both the ideology and the political apparatus he required to manipulate labor and to commit the populace to his revolution.

[II]

In the conflict-ridden society of Cuba, radical socio-economic doctrines reached a receptive audience, providing a militant core of urban workers and intellectuals with a unity of belief, purpose, and action. Anarcho-syndicalist, neo-Marxist, and Marxist beliefs had furnished that unity since the nineteenth century. These radical doctrines encouraged the development of the Cuban Communist party, one of the best organized, most active, and most powerful political blocks in Cuban history.

The development and successes of the Cuban Communist movement are closely related to the history and nature of Cuban society, as well as to the agro-industrial character of the local economy. Periodic economic crises, chronic unemployment, popular dissatisfaction with the role of foreign capital, anticlericalism and the weakness of the Church, the undemocratic character of politics, the power of the *caudillo* and the timidity of his opponents—all played their respective parts in the rise of Marxism and the Communist party.

The influx of American capital into Cuba after 1898 encouraged expansion of the sugar industry; even more important, it hastened the breakdown of the island's ancient rural pattern and provided a special impetus for the growth of radical and socialist ideas. With the introduction of foreign capital, Cuba rapidly assumed the urban character (53 per cent of the population in the 1953 census) which distinguished it from much of Latin America. Though sugar dominated the export economy, more persons had jobs in the urban processing, packing, and shipping of sugar than in its cultivation. This urbanization of Cuban labor brought with it a host of evils, including the sweatshop conditions common to industrial nations. In an attempt to improve their condition, Cuban workmen increasingly turned to labor organization and the use of strikes to enforce their demands. Socialists as well as anarcho-syndicalists, many of them Spaniards, were in the vanguard of these efforts. Thus Cuban labor rapidly developed a history of constant struggle against profit-minded employers who, until the revolution of 1933, imported cheap labor rather than pay a living wage to local workers.

From the beginning, radical doctrines carried wide appeal for labor, although organization began under extremely unfavorable circumstances. Not only was official and public opinion in Spain and Cuba hostile, but free labor had to compete with servile labor until the emancipation of the slaves in the 1880's and, after that, with the cheap labor furnished by recently freed bondsmen. To protect his interests, the free worker had to organize, and the opposition he encountered everywhere forced him to take an increasingly militant stance. The chronic unemployment inherent in the economy, which always threatened to leave him jobless, tended to confirm his opinion that his one defense lay in militancy.

The history of labor's efforts to organize was essentially the story of anarcho-syndicalism and the Communist party. Although the mass of workers was neither Communist nor neo-Communist, from the early thirties until the mid-forties labor achieved considerable gains under anarcho-syndicalist and, more significantly, Communist leadership. Its losses occurred in eras of non-Communist leadership—during the Machado administration and, later, under the Auténticos in the late forties and early fifties. In the world of labor, therefore, radical doctrines, including Marxist and Communist beliefs, often received a friendly hearing.

[III]

Radical ideas entered Cuba from Spain in the 1860's. Their champions were Spanish workers who had fled their homeland in search of economic opportunity and freedom from persecution. Most of the workers were poorly educated, apathetic immigrants, but there was a core of anarchists and anarcho-syndicalists—many of them from Catalonia, the heartland of radical doctrines—men committed to a belief in the inevitability of class warfare and of hostility between employer and worker. They began almost immediately to agitate for higher wages, better working conditions, and the right to organize trade unions. Until the Communists eliminated them from the scene in 1931, anarcho-syndicalists wielded a powerful influence in the ranks of Cuban labor.

The labor movement, not surprisingly, emerged from the tobacco industry and, until the 1920's, received dynamic and progressive leadership from tobacco workers in Havana. There, in 1865, anarcho-syndicalists established a newspaper, *La Aurora*, to voice the grievances of workers in the tobacco industry. One of the columnists of *La Aurora* was José de Jesús Márquez, an advocate of cooperative societies and a vague form of humanitarian socialism, who had lived and worked in the United States. In 1866, partly as a result of the activity of *La Aurora*, Márquez and his friends, including anarcho-syndicalists, formed the first labor union in Cuba, the Asociación de Tabaqueros de la Habana. Its prophets were Mikhail Bakunin, Errico Malatesta, Elisee Reclus, and Anselmo Lorenzo, whose views were disseminated to the rank and file through a system of "readers" the Asociación introduced into the tobacco factories. Other unions were subsequently organized in the industry, and in 1887, the First Workers Congress was convened, under anarcho-syndicalist direction, in Havana—establishing a central meeting house in the city, the Círculo de Trabajadores. In 1892 the unions sponsored a Regional Workers Congress which, among other things, called for independence and linked independence with social revolution.

Non-Marxist socialism thus arrived in Cuba in the last decade of the nineteenth century, after anarcho-syndicalists had won converts in the ranks of labor. Socialism of this type, frequently confused with anarchism by the Cuban public, was not entirely new to the island. Unorthodox thinkers had come into contact with it already. Miguel A. Bravo

Senties, a lawyer by profession and an adviser to Vicente García, a Cuban general in the Ten Years' War (1868–78), for example, had even urged his chief to work for a "Socialist, egalitarian State." Another early Socialist was Enrique Roig y San Martín, who died in a Havana prison in 1889. Socialism as a doctrine, however, did not win a popular following until later.

Labor, and later the intelligentsia, provided the openings for socialism in Cuba. The paths of the two crossed frequently. Socialism received formal expression initially in the Partido Socialista Cubano, which had a brief existence in Havana in 1899. Its founders were Ambrosio Borges, a tobacco worker who had studied socialist literature as a reader in the cigar factories of Key West, and the poet Diego Vicente Tejera, father of Cuban socialism. Tejera, who apparently became a convert to radical doctrines during his travels in Europe, had already established himself as socialism's leading exponent on the basis of his essay, *Un Sistema Social Práctico.* In 1898 Tejera published *La Victoria,* a pro-labor, radical journal that featured essays on socio-economic questions. He and Borges had known each other since their days together in Key West, where both had joined the local branch of the Partido Revolucionario Cubano. With the aid of sympathizers in the tobacco factories, the two combined their talents to organize the Partido Socialista Cubano.

After the demise of this party, Carlos Baliño, who had collaborated with Tejera on *La Victoria* and was known as the grand old man of labor's radical wing, organized the Partido Obrero Socialista de Cuba in 1904. Baliño, the son of a Cuban insurgent and later one of the fathers of the Cuban Communist party, had acquired his socialist views in the United States. When the Spaniards denied him a job in his native land, he emigrated to Key West, where he found employment in the local tobacco factories. Partly as a result of his inability to find a job in Cuba, an opportunity denied many Cuban workers, Baliño championed the cause of independence. With José Martí, he was one of the founders of the Partido Revolucionario Cubano. Also in Key West, Baliño had befriended Tejera. In 1898, after the Spanish-American War, Baliño returned to Cuba, where he launched his lifelong effort to establish a socialist party. His Partido Obrero Socialista survived only briefly but, undaunted, in 1906 he organized the Agrupación Socialista de la Habana from the remnants of the Partido Obrero and the Agrupación Socialista Internacional, in which he had figured prominently. The government suppressed the organization during the labor strife of 1911.

Despite their failures, Baliño, Tejera, and Borges left a legacy for others and sparked a growing militancy among the rank and file of labor. That militancy found expression in the labor strikes of 1902, 1907, and 1911 among the tobacco workers, the construction trades, and railroad men. In all of them, leaders of the tobacco workers, frequently of socialist or anarcho-syndicalist persuasion, participated. These strikes, furthermore, were at least partially directed at American-owned corporations.

Communist doctrines, as distinct from socialist concepts, probably entered Cuba after the Russian Revolution of 1917, again through the ranks of labor and the intelligentsia. But it was not until the depression years of the twenties and the Machado repression that the Communist movement won a foothold on the island. Its growth was slow even then. During the labor troubles of 1911 Machado, then Minister of the Interior in the administration of President José Miguel Gómez, had organized a Federation of Cuban Workers, which he and later administrations manipulated to control labor. Determined to break this puppet apparatus, the left wing of labor (essentially the leadership of the Havana Federation of Labor, which included anarcho-syndicalists, socialists, and

Communists) organized in 1925 the National Confederation of Cuban Labor (Confederación Nacional Obrera Cubana or CNOC). Parent and junior branches cooperated together for some time, but eventually the CNOC, which came under orthodox Communist influence, split with the Federation, in which Trotskyists set policy. The Partido Bolchevique Leninista, which the Trotskyists established, enjoyed a short life, while the CNOC survived.

In 1925, meanwhile, orthodox Communist leaders—influenced by Carlos Baliño, who in the intervening years had embraced Communism—joined Marxist students from the National University in establishing the Cuban Communist party. Julio Antonio Mella became its first Secretary-General. Mella and Baliño had met in 1923. Mella, a university student leader with "the face and figure of a young god and a magnetic flight of oratory," was an idol among his classmates and editor of the review *Juventud*. In their search for professional literary advice, Mella and his fellow-editors employed Baliño, then 77 years old, as copy-editor of *Juventud*. When Baliño joined its staff, Mella, a radical of neo-Marxist leanings, was preoccupied with university reform; his pet project was to get the professors to teach their subjects in class and leave politics to others. In the course of his association with Baliño, Mella became a Communist. In 1925 he was arrested by Machado on a bomb plot charge. When he resorted to a hunger strike in prison, he was deported to Mexico, where he became a leader of the growing colony of Cuban exiles plotting the demise of the dictator, and the editor of an anti-Machado publication. Early in January 1929, hired assassins shot and killed Mella in Mexico City, apparently on orders from Machado. His death enshrined him as a martyr in the lexicon of Cuba's youth and, unfortunately for the dictator, led them to take a more active role in the struggle to unseat him. When Mella's ashes were returned to

Cuba in 1933, huge crowds met the ship carrying the funeral cargo.

Machado, in the interim, outlawed the Communist party and either jailed its leaders or drove them into exile. Baliño, to cite the case of one of them, died in a Havana prison. The dictator's repressive tactics drove the party underground and kept membership limited to a few die-hards in Havana, Cárdenas, Cienfüegos, and Manzanillo. Aliens, mostly Spaniards employed in the light industries, made up its predominantly labor following. At best, therefore, the Cuban Communist party was a clandestine organ in the days of Machado, though its members were active in the National Confederation of Cuban Labor.

After 1931 the Communist party shifted its tactics, abandoning emphasis on select membership in favor of mass recruitment of workers in the basic industries, particularly sugar. Aided by the worsening economic crisis, party rolls increased from approximately 300 in 1929 to 3,000 in 1933, and to twice that number in 1934. Branches of the party, in the interim, appeared in all but one of the six provinces and in such basic industries as sugar, tobacco, and coffee. To recruit the young, the party created a Juvenile Communist League.

Why was the Communist party successful at this juncture? First, hard times made thousands of Cuban workers receptive to any group offering a solution to their troubles, for, with rare exceptions, the foes of Machado ignored the plight of urban and rural workers. The old politicians remained indifferent or hostile, while the ABC and the Directorio Estudiantil overlooked in practice the needs of labor. Second, the Communists courted labor assiduously, with a program designed almost exclusively for the benefit of that embittered and disillusioned segment of the population. Third, by organizing the CNOC, the Communists backed their promises with action, while calling for an "agrarian and anti-imperialist revolution" to destroy the latifundia pattern and return the land to its rightful owners.

The platform of the Communist-directed CNOC proclaimed that a fundamental antagonism divided the propertied classes from the workers. It urged labor to build a socialist state, to establish a dictatorship of the proletariat, to seize control of the means of production and distribution of goods, and promised to satisfy the "immediate demands of the proletariat, both industrial and agricultural," and to advance its "material, social and cultural betterment." As the ally of the impoverished urban masses, exploited rural workers, and Afro-Cubans, the CNOC promised to combat war and colonialism in behalf of the "Final Objective . . . the revolutionary overturn of the bourgeois-feudal imperialist regime, in order to emancipate the oppressed people and the proletariat of Cuba as a class internationally exploited."

The Communists capitalized on labor unrest to help oust Machado from office. In December 1932, at a meeting of sugar workers in Santa Clara sponsored by the CNOC, Communists encouraged the workers to strike and 20,000 left their jobs. A year later, in August 1933, urban workers in Havana, again with Communists participating, launched their own strike, which in less than a month forced Machado to flee. The strike began with the walkout of bus drivers on August 1 and spread rapidly to include nearly all workers. After Machado's police fired on the strikers, they grew more militant, sabotaging and looting food stores. By August 5 Havana lay in the grip of a general strike, supported by merchants and businessmen.

Concurrently, others, including members of the ABC and the Directorio Estudiantil, who belatedly accepted the banner of labor reform, carried the strike into the countryside. Demanding better working conditions, higher wages, and recognition of their unions, 200,000 sugar workers joined the protest. On August 21, 1933 the workers seized a sugar mill in Camagüey Province; in less than a month, thirty-five other mills had fallen into their hands, and by early September, 30 per cent of the country's sugar production was under the workers' control. Meanwhile, rural Soviets made their appearance at Mabay, Jaronu, Senado, Santa Lucía, and other centrales. Mill-managers were held prisoner; labor guards at the mills wore red armbands for uniforms; strikers fraternized with soldiers and police; and, at Antilla, a red flag fluttered over city hall, while Communist-led demonstrations in Santiago forced the mayor and the provincial governor to flee their offices. Never before had Cuba witnessed such labor unrest.

The intensity of the strike and the Communist involvement, says Alberto Arredondo, led Sumner Welles to hasten his mediation effort. The goal of the general strike was to rid the island immediately of Machado, but, writes Arredondo, Welles wanted to depose Machado by gradual steps and replace him with leaders he could influence. The strike troubles, which Communists helped to foment, compelled him to act with haste. Arredondo maintains that Welles, fearing social revolution in Cuba, even urged Machado to free Communist and leftist prisoners and to legalize the party if the Communists would order the strikers back to work. Machado released his Communist and leftist captives, but by then Welles had decided Machado could no longer govern the island.

In January 1934 another general strike, though less widespread and effective than its predecessor (but perhaps more dominated by Communists) swept the island. The protest focused on the conservative Batista-Mendieta regime that had toppled the government of Ramón Grau San Martín. Machado's departure and Grau's policies quelled the first strike: his troops put down radical and Communist protest, while his labor reforms pacified the workers. The Batista-

Mendieta coalition relied chiefly on force to defeat the strike of 1934.

With Machado out of the way, the Communists organized a Republic-wide effort to unionize Cuban workers. The general strike against the Batista-Mendieta administration, which began among the tobacco workers and eventually included nearly all of labor, permitted the Communists to consolidate their gains. Enrique Lumen believes that the Communists organized half a million workers. In addition, the strike that helped to eliminate Machado and install Grau in power gave labor permanent and temporary gains: employer recognition of workers' unions, acceptance in principle of the eight-hour day, workmen's compensation, better housing, and a ban on the closed shop in some industries.

Nevertheless, as the Commission on Cuban Affairs made clear in its analysis of the situation, the Communists were not responsible for the conditions that culminated in 1933 in the arming of the workers, the seizure of sugar mills, and the attempts to organize rural soviets. The Communists merely exploited a bad situation, acknowledging later that their activities in the Confederation had lagged behind the spontaneous protest of the workers, who proved more radical than the Communists. The Communists, nonetheless, emerged from the strife as the undisputed bosses of the labor movement.

The revolution of 1933, moreover, did not receive Communist party endorsement, nor did the regime of Ramón Grau San Martín. From the beginning, Communists opposed Grau, including his famous nationalization of labor law which, from their vantage point, represented the work of "petty bourgeois servants of landlords and imperialists." During Grau's four months in office, in fact until 1935, the Communists adamantly refused to cooperate with non-Communist leftists and directed much of their venom at Antonio Guiteras, the radical but non-Communist reformer in Grau's cabinet. Not till Grau fell did the Communists adopt their Popular Front line in Cuba, belatedly attempting to establish an alliance with the out-of-office Auténticos. When Grau and his supporters rejected their bid, they turned to Batista. For his part, Grau opposed the Communists, even permitting the army to fire on Communist demonstrators in Havana who converted the arrival of Mella's remains into an opportunity for political protest.

Yet Grau failed to convince Sumner Welles of the non-Communist nature of his regime—though his nationalist reforms were beginning to win for him the sympathy of the rank and file of labor which never had been Communist. Welles and conservative Cubans who tagged the revolutionaries with the Communist label were either mistaken or opportunistic in their charges against Grau. Only a small core of Trotskyists backed him and orthodox Communists warned that his reforms would invite United States intervention. However, clandestine Communist activity during the revolution, almost always the work of irresponsible hotheads, undoubtedly led to Grau's downfall. It seemed to support Welles's allegation that the administration "did not have effective control of the country."

Until the middle of 1936, the Mendieta-Batista administration adopted a tough anti-Communist stand and a hostile labor position. Then, confronted with the growing opposition of conservative politicians, Batista altered his tactics. Believing he needed labor support to remain political boss of Cuba, and that Communist leaders could provide that support, Batista joined hands with them. In 1937 he permitted Communists, socialists, and leftists to form the Partido Unión Revolucionaria (PUR), and in 1938 legalized the Cuban Communist party, banned since the days of Machado. In return, Batista extracted a promise of support from Communist labor chieftains who, for their contribution, received virtually a free hand with labor.

The alliance with Batista proved mutually beneficial. With the dictator's benevolent approval, the Communists reorganized the old labor structure, renaming it the Confederation of Cuban Workers (CTC). Batista, for his part, established a Ministry of Labor. The workers won increasing benefits, and Communist direction kept labor troubles to a minimum. Of the delegates elected to the Constitutional Convention in 1940, six were Communists, and their efforts to some extent account for the adoption of an advanced labor code. In the elections of that year, Communist candidates polled more than 80,000 votes, winning eight seats in the Chamber of Deputies. In 1943 Juan Marinello, a Communist stalwart, was appointed Minister without Portfolio in Batista's cabinet, and when he ran successfully for the senate in 1944, Carlos Rafael Rodríguez, another Communist, replaced him. In that election the Communists, under the banner of the Partido Socialista Popular (PSP), polled more than 120,000 votes and elected three senators and seven deputies, including Lázaro Peña, boss of the CTC. In this era, to quote Blas Roca, "Batista was the fountainhead of Cuban democracy," a man "with a heart that spoke for the people." However, Batista— the "people's spokesman" and the candidate backed by the Communist party—lost his bid for the presidency in 1944.

Communist membership, which stood at 43,000 in 1940, rose to 150,000 by 1946. In the election that year the party polled almost 200,000 votes, more than 8 per cent of Cuba's registered voters and over 10 per cent of the total votes cast. With justification Blas Roca hailed the election as a mighty triumph for the Communist party which, he declared, was now a major national political organization. In the Senate Juan Marinello was elected first vice president. The Communist newspaper *Hoy*, meanwhile, had one of the largest circulations in Havana, while the Communist-owned *Mil Diez* was the only free channel radio station in Cuba. In 1940, when Batista banned all "totalitarian propaganda," including that of the Germans, Italians, and Spaniards, he exempted the Communists. In April 1943 Batista's regime recognized the Soviet Union.

Under Batista, for the first time in Cuban history the Communists offered the worker a political party that truly represented the common man. Whatever its motives, according to the writer and scholar José Enrique Sandoval, the Communist party was largely responsible for the organization and discipline of the labor movement while, to Angel del Cerro, only the scrupulously honest Communists "had nothing to fear from good government." Of the Communist parties in Latin America, the Cuban organization alone received official recognition and sanction, the sole group to collaborate actively with the regime in power. By dint of hard work, "devotion, training and tactical skill—all of which qualities their bitterest enemies emphasized"—the Communists, in the opinion of the World Bank's 1951 *Report on Cuba,* "succeeded in attaining practically complete control of the Cuban labor movement." In the process, they molded "a relatively compact and disciplined urban proletariat," perhaps the one group in Cuban society acutely aware of its class interests— the result of decades of extremely effective popular education on the workings of an economic system by Communists and their predecessors, the anarcho-syndicalists.

The Communists, furthermore, offered the CNOC able leadership, first under César Vilar and Rubén Martínez Villena and, after 1934, under Blas Roca, a member of the shoemakers union, and Lázaro Peña of the combative Tobacco Workers Federation. Roca (Francisco Calderío) had joined the Party in the twenties and risen through party ranks by virtue of his organizational skills and political ability. He had directed the Party since 1938 and managed the successful political campaigns of the forties. Peña, in his role as union chief, became one of the most powerful men in Cuba. A big, handsome Afro-Cuban, ingratiating in manner and a forceful speaker, he rose to prominence as a cigar-roller in the tobacco industry and won a large popular following among the Cuban people. Of immense personal integrity, he reportedly returned to the CTC five of the six-hundred-dollar salary he earned monthly. Though a dedicated Communist in the days of Stalin, he claimed that Cuba and Cuban workers were his primary concern. By 1946 his skillful direction had placed most of the country's labor unions in the CTC, nearly all under Communist leadership. The rural adjunct of the CTC was the National Syndicate of Workers in the Sugar Industry.

It was this Communist-built political structure, and its concommitant hold on the rank and file of labor, that the Auténticos attacked and eventually dismantled. Hampered by his narrow victory at the polls in 1944, Grau at first tolerated Communist control of the National Confederation of Labor, despite the pleas of the Auténticos who demanded a purge of their old adversaries. Grau had to move slowly: his political opposition controlled congress, labor strife would have destroyed his regime, and the army remained loyal to Batista. So, like Batista before him, he arranged a compromise with the Communists, coming to terms with Juan Marinello and Blas Roca, their spokesmen. In return for a promise of support, Grau accepted Communist control of the CTC, appointed a Communist vice president of the Senate, and gave the Communist-dominated CTC $750,000 with which to convert the Havana Fronton into a Workers' Palace. After the 1946 elections, in which the Auténticos captured control of both houses of congress—partly with the aid of the Communists who backed their candidates—Grau decided to break with his allies, who had become increasingly critical of the corruption in his administration and of his open support of United States foreign policy.

The Communists, who had stilled their denunciations of the United States during the conflict with the Axis, had reopened their anti-American diplomatic offensive by 1946. In

Havana the Soviet Embassy, staffed by some fifty members, including the only foreign press attaché in Cuba, was the largest in Latin America. Business transactions between the two nations were minimal, however, because the Soviet Union purchased only a limited supply of Cuban sugar. In an effort to propagandize the attractions of life in the U.S.S.R., the Legation entertained lavishly and sponsored exhibitions of Soviet art and programs on the Havana radio stations. Local Communists, meanwhile, had launched a propaganda campaign against the United States, as Washington countered with its own anti-Communist program demanding that nations in the Western Hemisphere purge themselves of "subversive" Communists. To win Washington's backing, as well as to placate his Auténtico followers, who had not forgotten Communist duplicity in 1933, Grau turned on his allies. Having finally won political supremacy in 1946, Grau had no further need of Communist backing.

Grau entrusted the purge to Carlos Prío Socarrás who, as Minister of Labor, occupied a key post for any assault on the Communists. The issue which sparked the struggle between the two camps was the desire of both to control public education. In May 1947, during preparations for the Fifth Conference of the CTC, the Auténticos demanded that the Communist chieftains resign, but Peña and his allies rejected the ultimatum. The night before the scheduled first meeting, someone killed a Communist delegate; the authorities blamed the Communists and suspended the conference. The Communists, however, held their own meeting, reelecting Peña as Secretary-General and 24 out of the 47 members of the Executive Council. In retaliation, the Auténticos met and elected Angel Cofiño, an independent labor leader (whom they later expelled from his post), and an Executive Council of their own to head the CTC. In July, when the Communist-dominated stevedores in Havana went on strike, Prío dispatched troops to the docks, then ordered the Communists evicted from the Workers' Palace, headquarters of the CTC, on the grounds that the building belonged to the Auténtico-controlled CTC. Later in the year, Prío arrested Peña and 125 labor leaders and, ultimately, hundreds of other Communists. In Oriente, an army captain murdered Jesús Menéndez, Communist boss of the Sugar Workers' Federation and a member of the Chamber of Deputies. With the collapse of the Communist apparatus, the Grau regime officially recognized the Auténtico-backed CTC, which quickly absorbed the country's labor federations. The movement of the powerful Maritime Workers' Union into the Auténtico camp was followed by that of the sugar and tobacco workers. By 1950 Communists controlled only a skeleton labor organization.

Prío carried the Communist issue into the presidential campaign of 1948. His platform claimed credit for defeat of Communist labor leadership and his campaign speeches promised to "destroy the Communist party in Cuba." In May the government seized the radio station *Mil Diez* and two years later banned the newspaper *Hoy* from Cuba. The decline of the Communist party followed rapidly. In the 1950 elections the party lost its three senate seats, though in Havana it managed to poll nearly as many votes as the government coalition. Registration in the party declined to 55,000 in 1952 and to 12,000 by 1958.

Batista, who had recaptured power in a military coup and required diplomatic recognition from Washington to stay in office, had an even stronger motive than either Grau or Prío for accepting the State Department's insistence that Latin American regimes cleanse themselves of Communists. In October 1953, therefore, he outlawed the party; but he did not discard his old policies entirely. Evidence indicates that he permitted prominent Communists to join the ranks of his backers, perhaps believing that through them he could woo labor's friendship. As his Under-Secretary of Labor, Batista appointed Arsenio González, an old-line Communist. And in the latter days of Batista's rule, few Communists were arrested; Ruby Hart Phillips reported that Batista's Bureau for Investigation of Communist Activities remained strangely inactive. Angel de Cerro believes that the Communists constituted a clandestine force throughout the Batista era. In an attempt to check the influence of the CTC, Batista also established his own labor faction, the Bloque Obrero. Apparently he distrusted Eusebio Mujal, boss of the CTC and a former Communist stalwart of the Partido Socialista Popular who had abandoned his old comrades-in-ideology for the Auténticos in 1946, and later betrayed them for Batista. Ambitious and opportunistic, Mujal had acquired a fortune as a sugar planter. But the Bloque Obrero proved ineffectual, and recalling perhaps his successes in the thirties and forties, Batista secretly welcomed Communist support. He permitted them, for example, to regain control of the eastern sugar worker's federation, while other Communists joined Batista's Partido Acción Progresista.

In this manner, Batista ultimately won a large measure of control over organized labor, though, ironically, he had cast aside his former pro-labor policies. His success, therefore, stemmed either from the apathy of the labor masses, the generally high level of urban prosperity, or, more likely, from his tight control of labor bosses, among whom Communists were again evident. When Castro and the rebels of the 26th of July Movement issued their call for a general strike in April 1958, organized labor ignored their plea, content to continue under Batista. The Communists, for their part, helped to sabotage the strike, later declaring in their semi-clandestine publication that it had failed because the rebels had not formed a popular front with them. "They were," acknowledged Phillips of the New York *Times,* "perfectly correct."

Paradoxically, the Communists did not speak for a majority of labor. Only a fraction of labor sympathized with them, perhaps one out of every four workers, in a union with a membership of more than one million in 1958. But that fraction and its militant leadership represented a popular force that would rally quickly behind the call of its former chiefs. The Communist party had been the one enduring political organization of the era; none of the other political groups could match its record.

With the decline of the Communists, the Cuban labor movement lost much of its vitality. The Auténtico bosses, and later Mujal, proved unable to equal the performance of their Communist predecessors. Corrupt and opportunistic, Mujal and his allies never won a large and devoted following. Further, because the Auténticos, and later Batista, manipulated the unions for political ends, the workers tended to look upon their union bosses as political leaders, not as true labor spokesmen. To cite the *Special Warfare Area Handbook for Cuba,* the bureaucracy-burdened unions had lost both their ideology and their contact with the membership. They no longer represented a force for reform. Some unions even grew wealthy in their own right; the Havana Hilton Hotel, to illustrate one case, was partly owned by the restaurant workers' union. The Auténticos, in reality, had given Cuba a system of government-managed unions, while Communist direction had partly checked that tendency. Ultimately, the policy of the Auténticos undermined the position of organized labor, weakening the one cohesive force that could have opposed Batista in 1952.

[IV]

The Communists were not simply a power in labor circles. Communists and their sympathizers, Marxists of varying hues, and socialists had played a major role in Cuban intellectual life. Not only were Communist party leaders generally "men of intelligence, magnetism and integrity," to quote the Commission on Cuba, but the party "won the support of some of Cuba's outstanding intellectuals and that of a growing group of younger teachers, writers, and professional people." The Commission emphasized that the party zealots were a dedicated lot, a characteristic that made "for a unity and an assurance which stand out in a confused society and where almost every group is ridden by schisms of personal ambition." Much of that unity and spirit in the party stemmed from the intellectuals, whom the non-Communist intelligentsia respected for their literary and artistic achievements.

The history of socialist intellectuals runs throughout the life of the Republic. Socialism, Marxian and non-Marxian, had found a friendly audience in the intellectual climate of Cuba. Members of the intelligentsia had identified with labor; one of the earliest was the editor of *La Aurora* whose newspaper had crusaded in the 1860's in behalf of the tobacco workers. The poet and essayist Diego Vicente Tejera had pioneered in the development of Cuban socialism, while the novelist Carlos Loveira helped to establish the Cuban League of Railway Workers and Employees in 1907. Julio Antonio Mella, student, intellectual, and co-founder of the Communist party, had organized classes for workers in Havana, and the poet Rubén Martínez Villena had been a founding father and later chief of the CNOC.

In the twenties, amid growing nationalism and despair over the failure to mold a just society which the collapse of the sugar market engendered, Marxist doctrines won new followers in Cuba. Intellectual discontent nurtured a growing literary production, much of it concerned with local injustices. In their search for a rational explanation for Cuba's inability to cope successfully with its problems, intellectuals fell back on Marxist historical determinism which placed the blame for domestic woes on capitalism and imperialism.

Emilio Roig de Leuchsenring's historical interpretation of

the Platt Amendment was one example of this Marxist view of Cuba's problems. As a young man, Roig had joined the Communist party and participated in the struggle to unseat Machado. His studies, in the meantime, led him to believe that foreign intervention in Cuba's domestic affairs, an inevitable offshoot of international capitalism, set Cuban against Cuban. Washington and Wall Street, in Roig's version of history, controlled the island, and the present and future welfare of every Cuban. To court American backing—which each Cuban needed to maintain or to improve his position in society—Cubans had to compete with each other.

Roig attempted to demonstrate that Cuban acceptance of the Platt Amendment made a "beggar's role" inevitable for the Cuban. He concluded that no Cuban should accept in any form the principles of the Platt Amendment. He decried the opinion of those who believed the Platt Amendment neither limited Cuba's existence as a free, independent and sovereign people nor gave pretext for foreign intervention. To Roig the Platt Amendment was unacceptable under any conditions. The doctrine justified the pretension of the United States for acting as policeman in the Western Hemisphere, which Americans claimed as their zone of political and economic hegemony. The struggle against the Platt Amendment was not merely against a piece of diplomatic legislation, but against capitalistic exploitation of Cuba which the doctrine symbolized and justified.

In his early studies Roig had endorsed the opinion that a stable and progressive Cuba could circumvent the principles of the Platt Amendment. But as he looked carefully at the nature of the Cuban problem and applied Marxist logic and method to analyze Cuban history, he concluded that the island could never progress economically and politically as long as Cubans tolerated the Platt Amendment and the capitalistic system it symbolized. By the late 1920's Roig had become "convinced that in Cuba anti-imperialism [and, by implication, anti-capitalism] had to be, and was, synonymous with *cubanidad*."

The ideas of the first Republican-born generation, as Roig's dialectics illustrate and Francisco Ichazo stresses, were not merely nationalist but strongly impregnated with Marxist thought. The nationalist generation of the twenties discovered a Bible in Marxist ideology which led many young intellectuals to embrace it. Until recent times the beliefs of this idolized generation in Cuban history found receptive ears among the youth of Cuba.

Further, Marxist thought provided a certain universality for the Cuban scholar of humanistic bent. In Communism's denunciation of colonialism, the intelligentsia discovered a convenient rationale for the plight of local government and, in Marxist condemnation of American capitalism, a scapegoat for Cuban failures to establish a just society. In the opinion of so eminent a non-Marxist scholar as Enrique José Varona, for example, the Marxist theory which explained all social development in economic terms was no more than the truth in slightly exaggerated form.

A Cuban, furthermore, did not have to endorse Communism in order to hold ideas of Marxist slant. To Antonio Núñez Jiménez, geographer and professor, it was possible to be a leftist non-Marxist and still share common goals with Communists, for the issues were nationalism, imperialism, and reform. Ultimately, this unity of purpose and ideas helped Communists to gain acceptance, opening to them positions of prominence as intellectuals, labor leaders, and politicians. The climate of opinion permitted Communists to play a distinguished role in the intellectual life of a predominantly non-Communist country which, because of previous Marxist activity, had learned to tolerate, if not always accept, Communists.

From the early twenties Marxist intellectuals functioned actively in the fields of education and the arts. Mella edited

Juventud, a literary journal with wide appeal among students, while he and other militants organized branches of the Communist party in the National University, the Havana Institute, the Normal School, and the technical schools at Rancho Boyeros. Father of the Protesta de los Trece, the leaders of the anti-Machado protest of the intelligentsia, was the poet and writer Rubén Martínez Villena, chief of the CNOC until his death in 1934. *Avance*, magazine of the Vanguardistas, the intellectual mentors of the anti-Machado protest, had Communists on its staff—among them the Catalan Martí Casanovas and the poets José Z. Tallet and Juan Marinello—who rose rapidly through the ranks of the party. Other leading writers who joined the faithful were Salvador García Agüero, Antonío Macias, and Regino Pedroso, a factory worker whose poetry in the Batista era equated Marxism with idealism.

Marxists found an especially friendly hearing among Afro-Cubans who, shunned by white society and denied economic equality in practice, often proved eager converts. Local Marxists had prepared the ground well. As early as 1905 Carlos Baliño, then an advocate of socialism, had argued the equality of Negroes and whites. In the twenties, Marxists had hotly rejected the neo-Darwinian theories of social evolution which justified the exploitation of Afro-Cubans on the ground that social evolution, which eliminated the unfit from society, assured the steady march of society's best elements. Afro-Cubans, whose poverty distinguished them from their white neighbors, had been singled out for special condemnation. Marxist defense of Negro equality brought many Afro-Cubans into the Communist fold, the racial question thus playing a special role in the clash of ideologies in Cuba.

In the Marxist camp a number of Negroes rose to positions of prominence. Afro-Cuban Communists helped to establish the distinguished journal *Avance*. The Vanguardistas, intel-

lectual avant-garde of the day and patrons of Negro literature, included among their number the noted Afro-Cuban
poets Nicolás Guillén and Tallet. A co-founder with Fernando
Ortiz in 1923 of the Society for Afro-Cuban Studies and
father of the *negrista* school of poetry, Guillén employed
African themes to write bitter political indictments of the
squalid life of the poor, Negro and white, and to condemn
their exploitation by the rich and powerful. Another Afro-
Cuban scholar, Juan Marinello, received international acclaim as a student of Martí and as a thinker, essayist, and
fighter for social justice. He had a national following among
the youth of Cuba in the forties and, in 1958, ranked high
on the list of Cuba's foremost men of letters—a niche shared
by Guillén.

On the labor front, the Communists made thousands of
converts among Afro-Cubans. Some became union officials,
for example, Lázaro Peña, the most powerful boss in the
history of the island's labor movement. Another Afro-Cuban,
Blas Roca, spoke as the ideologist of the Communist party,
as well as a labor chieftain. Among Communist leaders who
survived the downfall of the 1933 revolution were the Afro-
Cubans Carlos Oliveras and Severo Aguirre, while a Negro
Communist, León Alvarez, led the most famous of the attempts to establish rural soviets in the sugar industry, the
Realengo 18. Jesús Menéndez, another Negro, headed the
Sugar Workers' Federation until assassinated in 1947. The
leadership of these men and that of other Afro-Cubans
encouraged the Communist party to pressure strongly for
racial equality—advocating even a separate Negro state in
Oriente—while Negro militants among the Communists
helped to persuade the Constitution-makers in 1940 to legis-
late racial equality. All in all, many Afro-Cubans enjoyed
influential roles in Communist ranks, either in the party or
in labor.

[V]

Cuban Marxists, in summary, had participated from the start in the Republic's history. Beginning in the 1920's, they wielded enormous influence in the labor movement, dictating its development and policy for two decades. In a sense, the story of labor's effort to organize, as well as union labor's successes and failures, is a history of Communist activity. On the intellectual scene, Communists shared in the literary and artistic life of the country, while Afro-Cubans discovered friends and allies among the party faithful who welcomed them into their ranks. Whether or not Communist activity weakened or strengthened the fabric of society, that activity is an indisputable fact of Cuban history.

8.

The Splintered Society

Cuba has dictatorships and constitutional masquerades simply because that is the way that the majority of the Cuban people want it.
HERMINIO PORTELL-VILA

[I]

To the surprise of scholars who, on the basis of their knowledge of Cuban history, predicted minimal socio-economic change on the Cuban scene despite Castro's victory, the Revolution moved with astonishing speed and spectacular political success. In a matter of months an agrarian reform law was not merely promulgated but carried out—over the strong protests of traditional interests with an unbeaten record of opposition to socio-economic reform. By the end of the first year of revolution the old rulers of Cuba had lost virtually all political authority, while professionals and other members of the supposedly growing "middle class" were beginning their exodus from the island.

In the light of past failures to carry out reform in Cuba, what accounts for Castro's accomplishments? Obviously no single explanation provides a full and satisfactory answer, but every attempt to explain the success of the Revolution must take into account the peculiar character of Cuba in 1958.

[II]

No coherent society existed in Cuba in 1958, no stable or well-knit structure but simply, as the sociologist Lowry Nelson noted, "a society in a state of emergence." The individual components of Cuban life did not constitute a nation. While Cubans were profoundly nationalist, their society—a collection of pieces held together by circumstance and historical accident—encompassed economic conflicts, ethnic rivalries, and rural-urban differences that mocked the myth of nationhood.

A number of factors determined the island's fragmented society. No permanent, homogeneous ruling class had evolved on the island. The local ruling group, continually in the process of transformation, established no true hegemony. Because Spanish feudalism never had taken root on the island, no traditional landed élite existed. The large sugar plantations dated back only to the waning days of the colonial period. For more than three centuries the land had been widely distributed; thus the relative insignificance of latifundia checked the rise of the Spanish feudal system.

Sugar and the influx of American capital further disrupted growth of the plantation common to the Spanish mainland colonies. Even the large estates left behind by Spain largely disappeared; therefore, no class of landed patricians in the pattern of Mexico or Peru, or serfs tied to the land and bound by law to the *hacendado*, characterized Cuba. An American-owned, agro-industrial unit substituted for them, fostering an entirely different relationship between management and labor and, in the process, eliminating the existence and need for an élite in the Spanish-American sense.

Recently Cuba had acquired a pseudo-aristocracy of bourgeois background whose wealth had been won by participation in the economic life of the Republic—a plutocracy, maintained the scholar J. F. Carvajal, which stepped into the breach when the Spaniards departed. This new group merged with the remnants of the old colonial élite, and both eventually joined hands with American investors who poured capital into the sugar industry after the Platt Amendment provided the necessary guarantees. On the basis of antecedents and values—a concoction of Spanish, Cuban, and American ingredients—the new plutocracy had little in common with an agrarian élite. Except for a high per capita income which distinguished it from less affluent groups, its ties were with the bourgeoisie. A neo-entrepreneurial clan lacking the élite's consciousness of unity and class and exercising only a limited leadership, this plutocracy in no sense controlled society in the manner of the élite of Peru or Colombia, which dictated not merely the economic, but the social and political system. Edmundo Desnoes, a contemporary Cuban novelist and writer who resigned as editor of *Vision* in order to return to Cuba in 1960, makes this point bluntly in his *Inconsolable Memories*. "That's the only thing for which I have to thank the revolution . . ." which, he writes, "really fucked up all the damned half-wits who hoarded everything here! I can't say 'governed' because they didn't have the foggiest idea of what a ruling class is all about."

The problem of defining and understanding the middle class raises nearly insurmountable difficulties. The lateness of independence, the monocultural system, the preponderant role of foreign capital, the sugar latifundia, and the absence of small industries—all these questions, as Carvajal indicates, markedly influenced the class structure of Cuba.

In his study, Lowry Nelson points out that outside observers might conclude that the Cuban social structure consisted simply of upper, middle, and lower classes. Such a definition, he warns, oversimplifies "a complex situation." If wealth and income are the criteria, Cuba undoubtedly possessed an upper and lower class. But, he emphasizes, a sixth sense advises him that Cuban society had not "set" or "jelled." The class variations between extremes of wealth and poverty make any attempt to generalize dangerous.

Instead of three groups, Nelson divides Cuban society into two major categories. In the top echelon he includes upper-upper, middle-upper, and lower-upper groups; at the bottom, he lists upper-lower, middle-lower, and lower-lower groups. The upper class embraces managerial people as well as office workers, and those "descended from upper-class families regardless of their present state of wealth and income." In the lower class, he places manual laborers and those "descended from families of this class." Cubans, according to Nelson's thesis, could not be classified solely on the basis of income—since income is of secondary importance in the subtle socio-psychological distinctions that make class identification difficult.

The problem of defining middle class involves, in essence, a question of attitudes. Was there a Cuban middle class with its own set of values? Because the middle groups identified themselves with the plutocracy and its values, Nelson concludes there was not. Rather, the middle groups wanted to resemble the upper class, to live in similar style, in luxury if possible. The distinction between rich and middle class was a difference in standard of living and not one of attitudes: the rich simply had more than the less affluent.

In addition, it is imprecise to speak of a national bourgeoisie, for the middle groups were almost totally identified with United States interests, corporations, and finance. They had few holdings of their own and few exclusively native interests to protect. As Boris Goldenberg argues, the spirit of anti-imperialism, a feature of any native entrepreneurial class, found no spokesmen among the Cuban bourgeoisie— especially after 1933, when United States trade and economic concessions drew American businessmen and the Cuban bourgeoisie closer together. Students and the intelligentsia even accused Cuban entrepreneurs of being pro-American.

Although it is an axiom of politics that an independent middle class is the product of native interests, the bourgeoisie, dependent on the foreigner, had virtually ignored the need to build native industry. Not until 1927 were fledgling industries even protected by legislation. Moreover, immigrants, particularly Spaniards who seldom accepted the island as their permanent home, weakened considerably the nationalist sentiment of the middle groups. True, the tide was beginning to turn; native Cubans were entering business for themselves, establishing a small but growing number of light industries and winning a larger share of the sugar industry. Domestic shoe production, for example, supplied more than 90 per cent of domestic demand, while textiles represented only 2.7 per cent of Cuban imports. Despite this belated trend, however, no basic shift occurred in the economy: imports of fixed capital goods, to use one illustration, had not declined but grown from 52.6 per cent in 1949 to 60.9 in 1958. Private enterprise was still largely foreign; educated Cubans, schooled mainly as doctors or lawyers, turned to public office for a livelihood, converting the national treasury into their chief employer. At the bottom of this nebulous class, an army of petty traders, entertainers, guides, and procurers—"bourgeois" in outlook and aspirations—exacted a living from the tourist industry and the tastes of the luxury-minded. Many had jobs only during the tourist season.

Nowhere was the weakness or nonexistence of the middle

class more evident than in rural Cuba. With 40 per cent of the population labeled rural and a far greater percentage dependent directly or indirectly on agriculture, the island should have possessed a rural middle class. It did not. Apparently, the *colonos*, renters, and sub-renters, as well as the foremen, superintendents, and mill-managers engaged in the sugar, tobacco, and coffee industries, which made up a sizeable population, formed a middle class. Close inspection, however, revealed that in practice these groups lacked an independent role of their own; they were at the mercy of the entrenched interests and, as such, resembled their urban counterparts.

In summary, the middle class did not exist as a class. It was a collection of groups, none with a clear concept of its place in society, but each imbued with a set of *petit* ideals, the sum of which did not add up to an ideal of class. Passive in its political attitudes, each group had involved itself in national issues only when threatened directly. No unanimity of opinion on national questions bound them together, especially on matters relating to the political and moral health of the country. In 1952 each group accepted passively Batista's coup, as each had bowed before the political chicanery of the past.

The lower classes were equally fragmented, united only loosely by the common bonds of poverty and want. A small, urban proletariat lived in the slums and shanty towns of Havana and other cities, their numbers swollen periodically by hordes of unemployed workers from the country in sugar's dead season. The jobs of the urban proletariat were mainly in construction, the making of tobacco products, public utilities, shipping, and those service industries closely tied to the influx of tourists. The field hands and men permanently employed in the sugar mills, tobacco *vegas*, and cattle ranches were their allies in the countryside. A minifundist group of 250,000 small farmers and their families, who eked out a precarious existence by cultivating an average of fifteen acres of land, nearly half as sharecroppers or squatters, lived on the fringe of the workers' world.

A labor force of 700,000 without jobs or only seasonally employed—almost double that of men with full-time jobs—colored markedly the structure of the bottom order. Approximately half had jobs during the *zafra*, or for a few months of the year in the construction business. To cite Robin Blackburn's perceptive analysis, this labor section "was not even exploited in the relationship of production; it was simply excluded altogether," it had no stake in society. All told, out of an employable work force of approximately 2.7 million, more than one out of four had no jobs, either for the entire year or a major part of it.

The index distinguishing upper-income from lower-income groups, the affluent from the poor and exploited, ran along rural-urban lines. Nearly everyone in the countryside was in the lower class, while virtually all upper-income individuals lived in cities and towns, in a land preponderantly agricultural in its economy, where three-fourths of the population depended on agriculture.

Rural residence and poverty distinguished a majority of the populace. An impoverished mass of unemployed or under-employed, a rural population identified with the cultivation of one crop, and a small urban proletariat—these were the major components of Cuba's lower class. Though laborers had banded together in labor syndicates, the harsh economic reality of the seasonable and unpredictable sugar economy undermined much of their organizational strength, in particular that of the sugar workers' union, the largest in Cuba. No social or ideological bonds held the workers together or integrated the majority of them into the structure of society. In this sense, the lower class had fewer loyalties to Cuban institutions than the amorphous middle groups. Embittered and frustrated, many workers had readily lent themselves to the machinations of agitators and reformers, whose main goal was drastic transformation of the society. Labor had even accepted workers' soviets for the sugar industry in 1933, while individual members of the lower class shared a widespread cynicism about each other, their government, their laws, and their country's future.

Nowhere was this distrust more glaring than in organized labor's relations with management. No mutual trust, no willingness to cooperate existed between the two, according to the World Bank's *Report on Cuba*. Labor and management blamed each other for the various ills that afflicted them. Though organized labor had made sizeable gains since the 1930's, the sentiment of its members was one of "revenge"— a response, concluded the Bank, conditioned by past abuses of management. Distrustful of their employers, workers ruthlessly exploited all advantages at the bargaining table, while their leaders rose to prominence "by displaying a maximum of aggressiveness."

In the Bank's analysis, the workers and their leaders were the victims of anxieties born of a stagnant economy, of the chronic unemployment that haunted their lives. An army of ill-housed and hungry men and their families were always there to remind the employed of the pitfalls that befell the victim who lost his job. Having suffered previously, the workers had little faith in the ability or will of investor and government to build new industries or provide additional jobs. Management-labor relations, meanwhile, were conducted on an impersonal basis. A legalistic approach, in which the human factor was usually absent, conditioned management's view of labor. Few of management's experts, lawyers in the main, had first-hand knowledge of labor conditions, either in their own industries or on a national level. The extent of unemployment, the cost of living in a given area, housing and health conditions—these considerations, all of supreme importance to the worker and his family—were

seldom weighed carefully by the experts and their employers. In the opinion of the Bank, labor-management-govern-
ment relations had reached an impasse in 1950. Without
marked improvement, Cuba could expect "progressive deteri-
oration" of its economic picture. It would find its ability to
compete in the world market dramatically curtailed while at
home production, employment, and income would decline.
As social tensions grew, rich and poor alike might easily turn
to a dictatorship to "solve" their problems.

Questions of color and race split society in other ways. One
out of four Cubans claimed Negro ancestors, either from
Africa or the West Indies. The census of 1953 acknowledged
that 27.2 per cent of the population was colored; the correct
figure may have been higher. Furthermore, despite apologists
for Spanish colonization who vehemently deny its existence
in the Spanish American empire, race prejudice—the Spanish
brand mixed liberally with ingredients imported from the
United States—divided the nation along color lines.

In general, upper-income groups were white; color dark-
ened at the bottom of the social scale. Manual laborers were
frequently of Afro-Cuban background, and nearly all men
of black skin were poor. The rural work force had a pro-
nounced African tinge, especially the cane-cutters and the
unskilled in the tobacco and coffee industries. Although it
would be a mistake to interpret Cuban society in the context
of North American racial attitudes, darkness of skin in Cuba
as in the United States tended to identify low social position.

The race question has enjoyed a prominent historical role.
It strongly influenced the movement for independence, delay-
ing its coming. While Simón Bolívar and José de San Martín
were winning independence on the mainland, Cubans remained loyal to Spain in the face of efforts by Mexico and
Colombia to liberate them. The Cuban census of 1817 tells
a good part of that story: blacks outnumbered whites, while
on the mainland only 2 per cent of the population was of

African stock. Cuba had more Negroes than the continental colonies of Spain, and until 1850 the growth of the Cuban population responded largely to the importation of Negroes. Alexander von Humboldt, the renowned German scientist who visited Cuba near the turn of the century, estimated that more than 90,000 Negroes were imported between 1521 and 1791. In the opinion of others, Cubans had smuggled more than half a million Negroes onto the island after Spain formally abolished the slave trade in 1820, nearly all with the connivance of the local Spanish captain-generals. According to some figures, approximately 650,000 blacks, all told, were landed on Cuban soil by the mid-nineteenth century. From that time on, the relative number of Negroes in the local population declined, until in 1899 the census reported fewer Negroes than in 1837. The movement for independence appeared only after the whites gained numerical ascendency.

As historians point out, distrust of the Negro frequently kept many would-be liberators loyal to Spain. Fearful of the role that "liberated" Negroes might have in a republic, local Spaniards and Creoles opposed independence or favored annexation to the United States before the Civil War. With the defeat of the Confederacy, the Cuban slavocracy turned its back on union, preferring to remain under Spain, as the events of the Ten Years' War testify. When Cuba finally won its independence, there were twice as many whites as blacks. In brief, color often divided patriots from loyalists.

Directly or indirectly, the Negro frequently supported the cause of reform. As the exploited laborer on the sugar plantations, he had persistently opposed the system, first pleading for his emancipation and then demanding higher wages and better working conditions. In the beginning the enemy was the white landlord, Spaniard or Creole, and later the foreign-owned corporation. When his master identified with Spain, the Negro accepted the cause of independence, fighting and dying for it, and providing a number of patriot leaders, among them the legendary mulatto Antonio Maceo. In the course of his history as a slave and later as a poorly paid cane-cutter, the Afro-Cuban frequently rebelled. In the nineteenth century, slave revolts broke out in 1812, 1827, 1843, and 1879, and in 1912, under the Republic, a Negro revolt erupted, led by Evaristo Estenoz, who claimed that his people had been denied equality. In the midst of Estenoz' efforts to organize a Negro political party in Oriente, the Independent Party of Color, fighting broke out between Afro-Cubans and government troops sent to suppress the movement. Some 3,000 blacks died in this race war, stirring animosities which did not subside for decades.

In the twentieth century, Negro protest, with the exception of the ill-fated revolt of 1912, merged with that of labor. Much of the labor trouble of the twenties and thirties had roots in "colored" Oriente, which suffered every affliction of the sugar industry. As cane-cutters, mill-hands, marginal farmers, or manual laborers, Afro-Cubans were the first to feel the pinch of hard times. A majority of the permanently unemployed or underemployed was undoubtedly of Afro-Cuban stock. The North American brand of race prejudice, which entered Cuba with United States capital and tourism, tended to aggravate the pattern of racial discrimination. At the social level, meanwhile, Afro-Cubans with distinctly Negroid features had little access to the best hotels and bars in Havana or the social clubs of whites.

Discriminated against in jobs and snubbed by the social élite, the Negro was, nevertheless, courted assiduously by politicians, particularly those out of office. From the time of Estrada Palma, first President of the Republic, whose Moderate party had the backing of the wealthy and of professional people, the Negro identified with the opposition. Hence, Afro-Cubans initially sided with the Liberals who promised them political and economic equality in return for their support. In practice, Liberals as well as Moderates and Conservatives feared the black multitude and kept it from winning political power, while they exploited the Negro's political naïvete for narrow and selfish ends. In 1920, to cite one notorious case, Menocal and the Conservatives wooed the Negro vote in order to elect Alfredo Zayas and thwart the Liberals, but to accomplish this end, they had to split the overwhelmingly Liberal Negro vote by reviving a feud between secret Negro religious sects. On their promise to espouse the Conservative cause, the *ñáñigos* (a voodoo clan) were permitted to parade publicly and perform their ceremonies without interference from local authorities. During the 1933 Revolution, student leaders of the Directorio Estudiantil, many of whom accepted neo-Darwinist racial concepts, tried to rally Negroes behind Grau's regime. Grau's social legislation won over many Negroes and mulattoes, but frightened whites who earlier had resisted their demands. For his part, Batista employed his own multiracial background to appeal for Negro support.

In 1958, nonetheless, it would have been an error to speak of a Negro population entirely outside the mainstream of the island's life. The Negro had enmeshed himself, racially and culturally, in Cuba. Nicolás Guillén, the noted Afro-Cuban poet, pointed out that the Negro had contributed immeasurably to the island's development. Economically, the Negro had been the backbone of Cuban life for centuries. Without him the great sugar plantations, which had rewarded their owners handsomely, could not have thrived. The entire background of the nineteenth century would have been very different had Africans not made the island their home. In Guillén's opinion, the African had created in Cuba a true mulatto psychology, an intermediate culture, the *Negri-blanca,* which formed the fundamental character of the Cuban people and which, in the mind of the poet, was neither black nor white but mixed and totally fused.

Yet the colored population, paradoxically, was too often an unassimilated element in society. Though racial discrimination in Cuba was less intense than in the American South, the Afro-Cuban had tasted the bitter fruit of inequality and had behind him a long history of protest, insurrection, and native leadership. An exploited minority, the colored population had few loyalties to the system, and little preparation for changing it by democratic or peaceful means.

[III]

A society split by wide income differences, in which rich and poor lived in separate worlds, where a pervasive spirit of mistrust set individuals and groups against each other, provided shaky foundations for its institutions. In reality, the infant Republic never developed institutions of its own. The laws, the courts, and the government rested on a colonial experience that left the Cubans unprepared to rule themselves, and on foreign models ill-suited to domestic conditions. The institutions were victimized by public apathy, corruption, and self-interest.

No institution mirrored more accurately the native scene than the political parties. In the beginning, three factions battled for supremacy on the local political scene: the Conservative, Moderate, and Liberal parties. Until the late twenties, they divided the public coffers among themselves and joined forces to prevent a successful attack on their monopoly. In the 1930's the Conservatives renamed themselves the Democratic party; the more status-quo minded among them formed the Republican party in the forties. In the meantime, the Liberals became allies of Gerardo Machado, a stigma that virtually destroyed them as a potent political force after his downfall. All were conservative parties of wealthy Cubans with little mass support. Their program eulogized private enterprise, "democratic and honest" government, and opposed Communism. Their platforms expressed regret for the passing of the "good old days," and when the chips were down, they preferred dictatorship to "chaos and disorder."

Opposed to the Liberals and Conservatives were the reform "parties" of the middle sectors. From the early thirties until the late forties, Grau's Auténticos headed the list of these parties. He and his followers challenged proponents of the status quo only briefly, and when they fell into line after accepting an accommodation with the older parties, Grau won the presidency in 1944 with the support of reactionary Republicans. Embittered by the turn of events, reformers organized the Party of the Cuban People, the Ortodoxos, who claimed the mantle of Martí for themselves. By 1958 the Ortodoxos had split into moderates and radicals. Apparently a rule of thumb dictated the course of Cuban politics: conservatives remained faithful to their banner, but reformers, both individuals and parties, eventually joined the enemy camp.

The protest of the fifties was against all parties for, as Leslie Dewart states, all parties were totally discredited. When Batista seized power in 1952, middle-sector government was in a state of virtual political bankruptcy. Party goals were the spoils of office and the public treasury, for distribution among party hacks and leaders. The parties functioned in a world of their own, independent of public demands and aspirations, where loyalty to the party, its members and its leadership, dictated decisions and the outline of political philosophy. No one, explained J. González Lanuza, more resembled a Conservative than a Liberal. Party leaders with whom members identified, and who had welded them together, enjoyed immense stature, for the parties were personalist organizations, directed and controlled by one man: if successful at the polls, by the president of the Republic; if not, by the man who aspired to succeed him. At the local level, the boss on his way up the political ladder or the *jefe político* dispensed favors granted him by his superiors in return for his support. Cuba's political history had been the story of such men: the Menocals, Machados, Batistas, and Graus. The *caudillo* ruled, the chieftain who put personal and party needs above political principles and ideology, who served the foreign investor and the affluent. In the history of the island, wrote Carlos Márquez Sterling, "the point that stood out was the reliance on the *caudillo* as an expression of the Cuban intellect." Not surprisingly, therefore, Cuba, with the exception of the Auténticos in the 1930's, had no party of truly national or popular scope. Fidel Castro stepped out of that setting.

On the political front, violence characterized almost a third of the Republic's history: the first decade of the twentieth century, the late twenties until 1936 and, again, after 1953. In the countryside the Cuban had turned to the guerrilla warfare he had utilized against the Spaniards in the Ten Years' War, in the period from 1895 to 1898, and against Machado and Batista. Rich and poor alike indulged themselves in the national pastime of terror.

The ABC, one of the island's legendary protest groups, was a case in point. Organized in December 1931 to battle the Machado tyranny, it employed terror to combat terror. Composed mainly of young men from intellectual and professional ranks, the ABC won national acclaim for its ability to intimidate Machado and his gang of hired thugs. All members belonged to one of three alphabetical cells, from which the society took its name. During its heyday, the ABC had 2,000 members who, in the words of Ruby Hart Phillips, Havana correspondent of the New York *Times*, were "pleasant-mannered, well-educated youths, despite the fact they were certainly murderers." Sick of the cynical generation of 1895 veterans who had run Cuba since independence, the ABC resorted to violence to combat political ills, meanwhile urging abrogation of the Platt Amendment and a gradual break-up of the extensive American-owned plantations. On the fall of Machado, the ABC dominated the short-lived Céspedes administration and, after Grau toppled Céspedes, focused its terror tactics on Grau and his allies, openly supporting the unsuccessful revolt against them in November 1933. The ABC, however, was not alone in its use of violence. After Batista's thugs shot Antonio Guiteras in May 1935, members of "Young Cuba," which had been headed by Guiteras, sought revenge by killing every man who had participated in the murder of their leader. Eddie Chibás, idol of Cuban idealists in the late forties, won his spurs as a young man by throwing a bomb at a streetcar in the days of Machado. Mobs in Havana looted stores and wantonly killed Machado's backers after the dictator abandoned the city.

Without an effective political apparatus, Cuba was left at the mercy of the army; its two national chieftains, Machado and Batista, had controlled more than half the Republic's history. Unlike the military in other Spanish American countries, where the army's ties with the élite often fostered an "unholy trinity" with church and landlord, the Cuban army had an unconventional background. It was of recent origin—a twentieth-century phenomenon dating back less than five decades—the progeny of American policy architects who, having watched a motley band of malcontents oust Cuba's first president in 1906, decided to build an army to prevent a similar occurrence in the future. In one of his last acts, therefore, Charles E. Magoon had provided for a permanent army. However, the rebels of 1906 had been veterans of the struggle for independence and members of the Liberal party which had popular sympathy. Thus, from the beginning, the army was a foreign institution and, in the eyes of countless citizens of the island, an enemy of true partiots as well as the tool of vested interests.

Magoon further muddied the situation by appointing as the army's commander-in-chief "Pino" Guerra, the very man who had captained the organized revolt against Estrada Palma. When Estrada Palma announced his reelection, so legend has it, Guerra, then a Liberal representative in congress, walked out, threatening to "seek justice somewhere else." To train him and to build a modern army, Magoon dispatched Guerra to France and the United States to study military organization and tactics, to make impossible a repetition of the kind of revolt Guerra had engineered.

Although a foreign institution, the military took on local characteristics. As the servant of successive administrations from 1909 to 1933, the army had cloaked itself in the mantle of its sister institutions from Mexico to Argentina. The "Hispanization" of the army began with Guerra. In 1912 President José Miguel Gómez had decided that his reelection alone could save Cuba from chaos, but he feared the army, for Guerra was a vocal supporter of Gómez' rival, Alfredo Zayas. To rid himself of Guerra, Gómez offered him a special mission to Europe and a lucrative reward. When Guerra adamantly declined, Gómez had him shot. Fortunately for Guerra, the would-be assassins proved inept and he escaped with a wounded leg. Not one to repeat a mistake, Guerra resigned, leaving his post in the hands of Gómez' closest friend. Later, Guerra embraced Gómez, and the two helped to thwart Zayas' presidential ambitions. Yet not until the advent of Machado did the army become the personalist body native to Spanish American politics. A military man himself, Machado transformed the army into his personal tool and, in the process, into the spokesman for the rich and well-born. Ironically, it was this pampered military that overthrew him in 1933.

When Batista and his sergeants, men of humble antecedents, ousted a clique of officers from control of the army, they created a wholly new military situation. As army boss, Batista granted commissions to 527 enlisted men; only 116 of the former 500 officers, those willing to accept a mulatto commander, kept their commissions. By deposing the officer clique whose background identified it with ruling groups, Batista divorced the military from the traditional power structure; by race and social position, Batista and his men belonged to the lower classes. Yet Batista's betrayal of the revolutionaries in 1934, who undoubtedly had majority sentiment behind them, destroyed what mass popularity the army had won in its earlier coup. Born of mutiny and betrayal, the post-Machado army became the puppet of Batista, a military establishment shorn of traditional ties with the élite, an opportunist, predatory army of professional soldiers of the lower class but devoid of any class loyalties, distrusted alike by the populace and the affluent.

Thus Batista's army found itself in an anomalous situation. It was not popular, yet its personnel by race and class had close ties with the poor. The army had a high percentage of Afro-Cuban officers, approximately one out of three. General Querejeta, a Negro, commanded the army in 1949. Such a military had few staunch defenders in the ruling cliques; nonetheless, the army had consolidated its position by siding with the vested interests, the enemies of reform. The plebeian army, therefore, was caught between spokesmen for the status quo who decried change in any form, and the populace, with which the army had bonds and which demanded change.

To keep his hard-won victory, Batista walked a tightrope: to placate his men, he increased the size of the army, raised the pay of its officers, and allotted to it a larger share of the national budget. He limited opportunities for graft but never cut them off entirely, gave the army a more active role in political affairs, and employed soldiers to carry out social reforms, even asking them to build schools. In this manner, Batista's army achieved a new image by the late thirties. But the *caudillo* never strayed far from the premise that led him to betray Grau. His army maintained the status quo, which placated native and foreign interests, and, in return, the plutocracy learned to live with the mulatto sergeant turned officer-politician.

After 1944 the Auténticos attempted to purge the army of Batista's cronies, but ultimately failed. Grau began the shake up, replacing Batista's chief-of-staff with an officer of his own choosing and shifting or retiring the military commanders of the six provinces. When Grau and Prío Socarrás quarreled, Prío launched his house-cleaning of the armed forces, ousting Grau's men and substituting his own. Prío had doubtful success, for army officers twice plotted his overthrow before 1952. The Auténtico purge of the military, obviously, had not paid dividends, for the coup that returned Batista to power was the work of the army. Yet the coup alienated the army even more from responsible public opinion. Hence, in 1958, its position remained unchanged; it was a personalist military force lacking close links with either the wealthy or the poor, without strong roots in the socio-economic structure of the island or in the life of the people. The strength of the army rested on arms supplied by the United States, which stamped the military as an alien force in the minds of nationalists.

The Catholic Church occupied an analogous position, because it had failed to act as a cohesive element, or to unite, as it so often did on the Spanish American mainland, the conservative, traditional forces in society. In Cuba it was merely another feeble institution with only superficial strength. True, the Church enjoyed a wide popular base in the 80 per cent of the people who were nominally Catholic. Approximately a tenth of them practiced their religion, however.

Compared to Peruvians, Colombians, or even Mexicans, Cubans were not a religious people. Thousands of them —including women, who tended to be more "Catholic" than their menfolk—had embraced the materialistic doctrine of Communism. In his study of the churches in the island, J. Merle Davis claimed that the Cuban, though raised in the Roman Catholic fold, was "outwardly an agnostic"; and according to Leslie Dewart, a Catholic philosopher who spent long years on the island, "The Church and any organized, institutional practices are to most Cubans . . . ridiculous and beneath contempt." Of the Spanish American people, then, the Cuban was the least Catholic in his practices and attitudes, in terms of his devotion to the Church, his support of it, and his aesthetic and social life.

Institutionally, the Church was especially weak in rural areas. The Spanish colonial clergy had never built a large number of churches in the villages and towns, and nothing was done to shift the emphasis after independence. Without churches, there was no substantial rural clergy, which left contact between priest, cane-cutter, and farmer to happenstance. Even on a national level, Cuba had just 725 priests for a population of six million, one for every 7850 inhabitants. In the end, observed Lowry Nelson, as an established, functioning institution the Church was "virtually nonexistent" in rural Cuba. In large measure, therefore, the farmer, *colono*, and field-worker had no major stake in the fortunes of the Church.

Racial questions helped isolate the Church even more from rural people. Much of the countryside, and certainly heavily populated Oriente, was of Afro-Cuban stock, but more than three-fourths of the clergy was Spanish, including nearly all of the hierarchy. The alien priests, therefore, failed to establish much contact with the Afro-Cuban population or to minister to its spiritual needs. Davis reported "no religious life" among Afro-Cubans. The inability of the

Church to respond or communicate helped to explain, at least in part, the survival of crude forms of African spiritualism in small Afro-Cuban communities. Thus the Church could not claim a rural army of the faithful, nor call upon the rural people either to defend the Church's institutional position or that of society as a whole.

Nor was the Church a national pillar of strength. Except for a small, loyal band of largely urban and upper-income faithful, the Church had no mass following. Unlike the Church in other Spanish American republics, where it successfully resisted lay criticism, the Cuban Church had lost its special standing. Church and state were separated in 1900 and, less than two decades afterward, divorce was legalized. Nor had the divorce law simply languished on the statute books. Thousands of Cubans had taken advantage of it. In the twenties Machado signed a decree liberalizing the divorce law on the pattern of Nevada legislation, hoping in this manner to attract divorce business to the island. Batista's own divorce in 1944 touched off a wave of divorces among army officers and politicians. A law enacted in 1900 had made marriage a civil contract, though the Cuban clergy had eventually prevailed on American occupation authorities to permit marriage in either the Church or civil courts. However, of the 107 municipalities polled on this change, 80 opposed it, as did three of the six provincial governors and all but one of the magistrates in courts of first instance. In relation to other Latin American countries, a surprisingly large number of Cubans belonged to Protestant congregations. The Masonic lodges in Cuba were the largest in all of Latin America; every major town had its lodge, while their membership, which included such famous names as José Martí and Antonio Maceo, invariably played leading roles in the political and economic life of their communities.

Historical factors underlay this picture. The quality of the colonial clergy had been poor; too often the hierarchy had staffed Cuban churches with ecclesiastical offenders from the mainland colonies. Since Church and state were united under Spain, the clergy had opposed independence, incurring the wrath of the patriot fathers and alienating majority sentiment on the island. Nor had the Church indicated any deep concern for the plight of the poor. As a Spanish institution, the Church was a bond between colony and mother country, a bond that must be severed if Cuba was to be free. No wonder, then, that debates over the Church question were among the most acrimonious at the 1901 Constitutional Convention, which abolished the state-supported Church and decreed freedom for all religious sects and, in so doing, liberated the island from the clerical issue that haunts much of Spanish America.

In summary, the Church, loosely allied with upper-income groups, its national position weak and virtually absent in rural Cuba, particularly among Afro-Cubans, was an institution with little vitality or inclination to support reformers. Only a minority of lay Catholics opposed Batista; while one of the cardinals of the Church, Manuel Arteaga, traveled to the National Palace to congratulate the *caudillo* on his coup. The Church could not hold society together or rally public opinion, either in self-interest or on behalf of the status quo.

Despite the splintered nature of society, unity existed, a unity reflecting growing awareness of what it meant to be Cuban, and of Cuba's destiny as a people. In the 1920's a wave of nationalism engulfed the island; subdued in the forties, nationalism was on the move again by 1958, with a militancy of its own among the intelligentsia and the youth of Cuba. The result of years of frustration, of hopes dashed before they were reality, the new nationalism voiced popular aspirations for a society free of the old evils and the foreigner. The new nationalism advocated the return of the land to its native owners, diversification of agriculture, and industrialization. Believers dreamt of liberating the people from the foreign yoke, on which they placed the burden of responsibility for past failures. And the yoke, in their minds, was the United States.

[III]

This, then, was the structure of Cuban society in 1958. Cuba was a country with an affluent layer closely identified with American capital at the top and, at the bottom of the social scale, a large working mass, often exploited but better off than its counterparts in Spanish America. In between, amorphous middle groups existed, all striving to keep up appearances with the rich and equally dependent on foreign markets and imports. Neither the army nor the Church played its accustomed Spanish American role, though both were loosely tied to the status quo. Of the political parties none, with the exception of the Communists, had managed to build a tough, disciplined organization; none had survived the rigors of the Batista dictatorship of the fifties. Organized labor, in the interim, had succumbed to the venality of the times, which were increasingly difficult for hundreds of thousands of workers whose livelihood depended on the fickle sugar industry.

9.

The Making of a Revolution

Revolutions are not made; they come.
A revolution is as natural a growth
as an oak. It comes out of the past.
Its foundations are laid far back.
WENDELL PHILLIPS

Why, in summary, did Cuba experience a successful revolution in 1959?

It seems probable that the Cuban Revolution developed because a number of the conditions were present that have almost always characterized prerevolutionary societies. In terms of Crane Brinton's famous study of the revolutionary process, Cuban society shared certain "uniformities" with old regimes in England, the United States, France, and Russia, that had suffered revolutions.

To use Brinton's first of five "uniformities," these societies were not unprosperous but, on the contrary, upward-bound societies, where revolutionary elements were more annoyed or restrained than oppressed. The revolutions did not emerge from hungry and miserable people without hope of change. In comparison with other Spanish American peoples, Cubans were well off, particularly the middle sectors, which were among the largest in Latin America. However, although middle-sector politicians had wielded political power since the forties, the majority of individuals in the middle sectors had no voice in government during the Batista years. Revolutions, to cite Chalmers Johnson, occur in societies that have suffered change, but still demand further change.

Moreover, sharp class conflict characterized Cuba's pre-revolutionary society, though not in simplistic Marxist terms. Discontent centered in the middle sectors which, to employ Brinton's analysis, had "made money, or at least . . . have enough to live on, and who contemplate bitterly the imperfections of . . . [the] socially privileged." As he puts it, "Revolution seems more likely when social classes are close together than when they are far apart." But not only were the middle sectors restless; organized labor, a large and potent political force since the late 1930's, claimed a long history of violent struggles against both foreign and domestic employers.

Further, the dependent sugar economy had given a special character to Cuban society which made it vulnerable to the attack of a militant and committed minority. The welfare of nearly every segment of the population rested precariously on the production of sugar or, indirectly, on the importation for resale of American manufactured goods purchased almost entirely with the profits from sugar sales in the United States. For the great majority of workers, sugar dictated a predictable seasonal pattern, cycles of jobs and of unemployment based on sugar sales abroad. When harvests were good and markets abundant, there were well-paid jobs for the workers, but when sugar prices fell on evil days, wages dropped. Insecurity and discontent, therefore, were salient features of the worker's life in Cuba.

Nor did the old regime have a strong set of "native" values with which to defend itself. To use David Riesman's terminology, the island's society was "other directed"; social, economic, and value patterns were derived from outsiders. The middle sectors were particularly dependent and imitative. No independent middle class existed with a consciousness of class or an identity of its own. Instead of a national bourgeoisie, there were "international" middle sectors economically and even culturally dependent upon the United States for survival. Because infant Cuban industries employed only a fraction of the population, only a small minority of "middle class" Cubans engaged in activities dissociated from American interests.

Meanwhile, the old rulers of Cuba, essentially the sugar men, had become ineffectual politically, accepting passively the Batista coup of 1952 and later—some of them at least —supporting the anti-Batista protest largely out of inability to propose solutions of their own. In Brinton's terms, the old rulers of Cuba had lost faith in their ability to rule and the moral vigor required to control political life on the island. Many of the old class had become dissolute, succumbing to immoral ways in their personal lives, and consequently were politically inept.

Like the middle sectors, the plutocracy had little coherence as a class, being utterly dependent on foreign interests. Sugar, the lifeblood of the plutocracy, had almost no future outside the American orbit. Largely a phenomenon of the post-independence era, the plutocracy possessed few roots in the colonial past to equate it with the powerful and traditional ruling élites of the South American republics. National welfare for the plutocracy had narrow limits, circumscribed by the needs of the domestic sugar industry and the demands of American foreign policy. These needs of the plutocracy frequently clashed with the aspirations of youth and the aims of nationalistic intellectuals.

Furthermore, governmental machinery had broken down, partly because the old institutions had never fully achieved stability and partly because they were unresponsive to the economic problems posed by a declining sugar economy, problems which had bred dissatisfaction at almost every level of Cuban society. A governmental apparatus which had responded to the reality of politically primitive conditions during the first three decades of the Republic's life proved ineffectual in dealing with the demands of social classes eager to implant both political and economic reforms. One reason revolution takes place, Chalmers Johnson reminds us, is that "nonrevolutionary change" has failed.

Politically, Cuba was an immature society, with weak and unstable institutions and political parties that represented the will of *caudillos* or political cliques. Local government was conspicuous by its absence, while at every level party politics commanded decisions. Honesty in public life was a rare virtue as liberals, moderates, and conservatives vied with each other for an opportunity to plunder the national exchequer. Middle-sector rule—that panacea of many political scientists—had proved an illusion, for middle-sector government in Cuba was inefficient, corrupt, and nonrepresentative.

Nonpolitical institutions fell into the familiar mold. All had failed to provide a basis for unity for Cuba's fragmented society. The Catholic Church, largely urban and Spanish, had a tenuous hold on the population; rural dwellers and Afro-Cubans especially played only a marginal role in the Church. Except for a privileged minority, most Cubans paid no more than lip-service to the Church. Labor unions were essentially government-run and government-controlled, responsive not to the demands of their membership but to politicians. The army was the personal tool of Batista, with little or no support in the population at large or in the monied classes.

The intelligentsia, moreover, formed a bitter, restless, and alienated minority in society. Denied a voice in government and hostile to the values of the money-oriented middle sectors, to which most of them originally belonged, they voiced an increasingly negative view of Cuban society, much of which embodied their denunciations of the sugar economy and its ties with the United States. The intelligentsia's attack on the political structure of Cuba revealed not merely a discontent with Batistianos, Auténticos, and old *politicos* alike, but general disenchantment with the political principles of the old regime.

One by-product of this alienation was the participation of intellectuals in the ranks of the Communist party. Partly out of a sense of despair and partly because of the promise of socialism to provide a more equitable and moral society for the future which, says Denis W. Brogan, was "the great emotional strength of socialism, the force that won it so many supporters of the first rank in the last century," Cuban intellectuals helped to build an efficient Communist party apparatus and a unified labor movement. In the history of Cuban party politics only the Auténticos of the thirties managed to win a more genuinely popular following than the Communists and their intellectual allies. Ultimately, the Communist party provided Fidel Castro with the political organization, discipline, and goals he sorely needed when his loosely knit and heterogeneous 26th of July Movement began to disintegrate after the victory of 1959.

But in addition to the "uniformities" that it shared with the prerevolutionary societies of England, the United States, France, and Russia, Cuban society displayed revolutionary symptoms of its own. After all, as Chalmers Johnson stresses, a particular revolution must be studied within the context of the social system in which it develops.

For one, the Revolution of 1959 was made possible by Cuba's own revolutionary tradition. Since the middle of the nineteenth century every generation of Cubans had experienced revolution. Political and social turmoil had engulfed the island approximately every twenty-five years: the Ten Years' War of 1868 to 1878, the struggle for independence that began in 1895, and the revolution of 1933. Between 1902 and 1920 the island suffered at least two political revolutions which, though limited in objectives, disrupted peace and order. On the basis of Cuban history, the Cubans could rightly claim the right—indeed the obligation—to revolt in order to eliminate old grievances.

Second, a strident nationalism that placed the blame for many of Cuba's troubles on United States foreign policy, and on a sugar industry that relied on American capital and markets, provided a rallying cry around which Cubans of diverse backgrounds could be united. Nationalism offered Castro the means by which to win popular backing, endorsement of his drastic reforms, and support in his battle against the allies of the United States on the island. Anti-American nationalism thrived especially among intellectuals who were convinced that to achieve true freedom—an increasingly popular aspiration—Cuba must drastically modify or sever its traditional relations with the United States.

Finally, in Fidel Castro the Cubans discovered an extraordinarily gifted political prophet and leader who, with his bold challenge to Batista, not only captured the imagination and loyalty of the young but in the process managed to clothe himself with the mantle of José Martí, first of the great Cuban revolutionary figures. Undoubtedly the political and economic conditions in Cuba paved the way for Castro's surprising success, but the Revolution would have been vastly different without the leadership of this quixotic and charismatic man.

Bibliography

BOOKS AND PAMPHLETS

ABC, *El ABC al Pueblo de Cuba: manifiesto-programa.* Havana, 1934.

Acuña, Juan A. *Cuba: revolución traicionada.* Montevideo, 1962.

Aguilar León, Luis. *Pasado y ambiente en el proceso cubano.* Havana, 1957.

Alienes Urosa, Julian. *Características fundamentales de la economía cubana.* Havana, 1950.

―――. *Economía de post-guerra y desempleo.* Havana, 1946.

American University, Foreign Area Studies Division. *Special Warfare Area Handbook for Cuba.* Washington, 1961.

Andrade, Ramiro. *Cuba, el vecino socialista.* Bogotá, 1961.

Arredondo, Alberto. *Cuba: tierra indefensa.* Havana, 1945.

―――. *El Negro en Cuba.* Havana, 1939.

Arrom, José J. *Historia de la literatura dramatica cubana.* New Haven, 1944.

Atkins, Edwin F. *Sixty Years in Cuba.* Cambridge, 1926.

Baliño, Carlos. *Verdades del socialismo.* Havana, 1941.

Ballou, Maturin M. *Due South, Cuba Past and Present.* New York, 1885.

Barro y Segura, Antonio. *The Truth about Sugar in Cuba.* Havana, 1943.

Batista, Fulgencio. *Respuesta.* Mexico, 1960.

———. *The Growth and Decline of the Cuban Republic.* New York, 1964.

Beals, Carleton. *The Crime of Cuba.* Philadelphia, 1933.

Brinton, Crane. *The Anatomy of Revolution.* New York, 1938.

Brogan, Denis W. *The Price of Revolution.* London, 1951.

Brown, Wenzell. *Angry Men—Laughing Men.* New York, 1947.

Bustamante, Luis J. *Enciclopedia popular cubana.* Havana, 1948.

Calderío, Francisco (Blas Roca). *A que Partido afiliarse.* Havana, 1947.

———. *¡Al Combate! ¡Por la economía y el bienestar popular!* Havana, 1946.

———. *Católicos y Comunistas.* Havana, 1940.

———. *El socialismo cubano y la revolución de Fidel.* Lima, Peru, 1961.

———. *El triunfo popular en las elecciones.* Havana, 1946.

———. *Los fundamentos del Socialismo en Cuba.* Havana, 1962.

Carbonell, Néstor. *Guaimaro, 10 de abril de 1869—10 de abril de 1910. Reseña histórica de la Primera Asamblea Constituyente y Primera Cámara de representantes de Cuba.* Havana, 1919.

Carbonell, Walterio. *Crítica: cómo surgió la cultura nacional.* Havana, 1961.

Chadbourne, Thomas L. *Cuba and Sugar Stabilization.* Charlottesville, 1931.

Chapman, Charles E. *A History of the Cuban Republic.* New York, 1927.

Chester, Edmund A. *A Sergeant Named Batista.* New York, 1954.

Collazo, Enrique. *Cuba heróica.* Havana, 1912.

Commission on Cuban Affairs. *Problems of the New Cuba.* New York, 1935.

Cue Cánovas, Agustín. *Martí, el escritor y su época.* Mexico, 1961.

Dalton, John E. *Sugar, A Case Study of Government Control.* New York, 1937.

Davis, Merle J. *The Cuban Church in a Sugar Economy.* New York, 1942.

Desnoes, Edmundo. *Inconsolable Memories.* New York, 1967.

Dewart, Leslie. *Christianity and Revolution: The Lesson of Cuba.* New York, 1963.

Draper, Theodore. *Castro's Revolution, Myths and Realities.* New York, 1962.

Firmat, Pedro. *Bocetos (artículos sobre economía nacional).* Havana, 1931–1936.

Fitzgibbon, Russell H. *Cuba and the United States, 1900–1935.* Menasha, Wisconsin, 1935.

Foner, Philip S. *A History of Cuba and Its Relations with the United States,* 2 vols. New York, 1963.

Friedlaender, Heinrich E. *Historia económica de Cuba.* Havana, 1944.

García Kohly, Mario. *Grandes hombres de Cuba.* Madrid, 1930.

Goldenberg, Boris. *The Cuban Revolution and Latin America.* New York, 1965.

Government of Cuba. *Cuba's Three Year Plan.* Havana, 1937.

Gray, Richard B. *José Martí, Cuban Patriot.* Gainesville, 1962.

Guerra y Sánchez, Ramiro. *Filosofía de la producción cubana (agrícola e industrial).* Havana, 1944.

————. *Historia de Cuba.* Havana, 1922.

————. José M. Pérez Cabrera, Juan J. Remos, Emeterio S. Santovenia, eds. *Historia de la nación cubana,* 10 vols. Havana, 1952.

————. *Manual de la historia de Cuba.* Havana, 1938.

Guerra y Sánchez, Ramiro. *Sugar and Society in the Caribbean: An Economic History of Cuban Agriculture.* New Haven and London, 1964.

Guggenheim, Harry F. *The United States and Cuba.* New York, 1934.

Gutiérrez, Viriato. *The World Sugar Problem.* London, 1935.

Henríquez, Enrique C. *Problemas del nacionalismo revolucionario de Cuba.* Havana, 1941.

Herring, Hubert C. *A History of Latin America.* New York, 1961.

Hostos, Eugenio M. *Obras completas: temas cubanos,* IX. Havana, 1939.

Iduarte, Andrés. *Martí, escritor.* Havana, 1951.

Illán, José M. *Facts and Figures of an Economy in Ruins.* Miami, 1964.

Infiesta, Ramón. *El pensamiento político de Martí.* Havana, 1953.

International Bank for Reconstruction and Development. *Report on Cuba.* Baltimore, 1951.

Jenks, Leland H. *Our Cuban Colony.* New York, 1929.

Johnson, Chalmers. *Revolutionary Change.* Boston and Toronto, 1966.

Lizaso, Félix. *Panorama de la cultura en Cuba.* Mexico, 1949.

————. *Posibilidades filosóficas en Martí.* Havana, 1935.

Llaguno y Ubieta, Pedro P. *Bosquejo sintético del latifundio en Cuba.* Havana, 1930.

Lockmiller, David A. *Magoon in Cuba.* Chapel Hill, 1938.

Lumen, Enrique. *La revolución cubana (1902–1934).* Mexico, 1934.

MacGaffey, Wyatt and Barnett, Clifford R. *Twentieth-Century Cuba.* New York, 1965.

Machado, Luis. *Necesidad de adoptar una política de comercio exterior.* Havana, 1929.

————. *La enmienda Platt.* Havana, 1922.

Macoin, B. *Latin America: the Eleventh Hour.* New York, 1962.

Mañach, Jorge. *Martí el apostol.* Buenos Aires, 1944.

Manrara, Luis V. *Cuba Disproves the Myth that Poverty is the Cause of Communism.* Miami, 1963.

Marinello, Juan. *Consideraciones sobre el momento americano.* Buenos Aires, 1946.

——. *Ocho notas sobre Aníbal Ponce.* Santa Clara, Cuba, 1961.

——. *Revolución y universidad.* Havana, 1960.

——. *The Philosophy of José Martí and Our Socialist Revolution.* Ottawa, 1962.

Márquez Sterling, Carlos. *Discursos.* Havana, 1938.

—— and Manuel Márquez Sterling. *Proceso histórico de la Enmienda Platt.* Havana, 1941.

Martí, José. *Argentina y la Primera Conferencia Panamericana.* Buenos Aires, 1955.

——. *Cartas políticas: selección.* Havana, 1953.

——. *Diario de José Martí, de cabo haitiani a Dos Ríos (9 de abril a mayo 17 de 1895).* Ceiba del Agua, 1941.

——. *Discursos revolucionarios.* Havana, 1953.

——. *Esquema ideológica.* Mexico, 1961.

——. *Nuestra América.* Buenos Aires, 1939.

Martínez, Marcial. *Cuba, la verdad de su tragedia.* Mexico, 1958.

Martínez Bello, Antonio. *Ideas sociales y económicas de José Martí.* Havana, 1940.

Martínez Fraga, Pedro. *Speech Delivered at the Opening of the Cuban Pavilion, New York World's Fair, May 20, 1939.* Washington, 1939.

Martínez Ortiz, Rafael. *Los primeros años de independencia.* Paris, 1921.

Mella, Julio A. *La lucha revolucionario contra el imperialismo.* Havana, 1940.

Minneman, Paul G. *The Agriculture of Cuba.* Washington, 1943.

Nelson, Lowry. *Rural Cuba.* Minneapolis, 1950.

Onís, Juan de. *The America of José Martí: Selected Writings.* New York, 1953.

Ortiz, Fernando. *Contrapunto cubano del tabaco y el azucar.* Havana, 1940.

————. *Las responsibilidades de los Estados Unidos en los males de Cuba.* Washington, 1932.

————. *Los factores humanos de la cubanidad.* Havana, 1940.

————. *Martí y las razas.* Havana, 1953.

Phillips, Ruby H., *Cuba, Island of Paradox.* New York, 1959.

————. *Cuban Sideshow.* Havana, 1935.

Poppino, Rollie E. *International Communism in Latin America.* Glencoe, 1964.

Portell-Vilá, Herminio. *Historia de Cuba en sus relaciones con los Estados Unidos y España,* 4 vols. Havana, 1938–1941.

————. *Narciso López y su época.* Havana, 1930.

————. *The Non-Intervention Pact of Montevideo and American Intervention in Cuba.* Havana, 1935.

Portuondo, José A. *Bosquejo histórico de las letras cubanas.* Havana, 1960.

————. *El Contenido social de la literatura cubana.* Mexico, 1944.

Quesada y Miranda, Gonzalo, ed. *Obras completas de Martí,* 60 vols., IX, XVIII, and XXVII–XL. Havana, 1936–1942.

Rauf, Mohammed A. *Cuban Journal.* New York, 1964.

Remos y Rubio, Juan N. J. *Proceso histórico de las letras cubanas.* Madrid, 1958.

Rivero Muñíz, José. *Carlos Baliño.* Comisión Nacional de la UNESCO, 1962.

————. *El movimiento laboral cubano durante el periodo 1906–1911.* Universidad de las Villas, Cuba, 1962.

Rivero Muñíz, José. *El Primer Partido Socialista cubano*, Universidad de las Villas. Cuba, 1962.

Roig de Leuchsenring, Emilio. *1895 y 1898: dos guerras cubanas; ensayo de revolución*. Havana, 1945.

————. *El internacionalismo anti-imperialista en la obra política revolucionaria de José Martí*. Havana, 1935.

————. *El manifiesto de Montecristi: sus finalidades y proyecciones*. Havana, 1957.

————. *La revolución de Martí*. Havana, 1941.

————. *Los grandes movimientos políticos cubanos en la república: ingerencia, reacción, nacionalismo*. Havana, 1943.

————. *Martí, anti-imperialista*. Havana, 1953.

————. *Pensamiento político. Martí: síntesis de su vida*. Havana, 1953.

Saco, José A. *Colección de papeles científicos, históricos, políticos y de otros ramos sobre la Isla de Cuba*. Paris, 1858.

————. *Historia de la esclavitud de los Indios en el Nuevo Mundo*. Havana, 1932.

Schweyer, Alberto L. *La crisis del patriotismo*. Havana, 1929.

Segunda Asamblea Nacional del Partido Socialista Popular. *Los Socialistas y la realidad cubana*. Havana, 1944.

Smith, Robert F. *The United States and Cuba; Business and Diplomacy, 1917–1960*. New York, 1960.

Sociedad Económica de Amigos del País, Sesión solemne commemorativa del 141° aniversario de su función. Havana, 1934.

Sosa de Quesada, Arístedes. *Por la democracia . . . y por la libertad*. Havana, 1943.

Strode, Hudson. *The Pageant of Cuba*. New York, 1934.

Tejera y García, Diego V. *Soberanía de las convenciones*. Matanzas, Cuba, 1928.

Torriente, Cosme de la. *Cuba y los Estados Unidos*. Havana, 1929.

―――. *En defensa de los derechos del hombre y del ciudadano*. Havana, 1930.

―――. *La Enmienda Platt y el tratado permanente*. Havana, 1930.

Unión Social Económica de Cuba, *The Fourth of July in Cuba*. Havana, 1938.

―――. *Commercial Relations Between Cuba and the United States*. Havana, 1936.

U. S. Department of Commerce. *Investment in Cuba*. Washington, 1956.

Varona, Enrique J. *De la colonia a la república*. Havana, 1917.

―――. *La política cubana de los Estados Unidos*. New York, 1897.

Vitier, Medardo. *La filosofía en Cuba*. Mexico, 1948.

Wood, Bryce. *The Making of the Good Neighbor Policy*. New York, 1961.

ARTICLES

Alienes Urosa, Julián. "Evolución de la economía cubana en postguerra," *Trimestre Económico*, XVII (April-June, 1950).

Beals, Carleton. "Blackjacking Cuban Labor," *The Christian Century* (August 21, 1957).

Blackburn, Robin. "Prologue to the Cuban Revolution," *New Left Review* (October, 1963).

Bonsal, Philip W. "Cuba, Castro and the United States," *Foreign Affairs*, XLV (January, 1967).

Carvajal, Juan F. "Observaciones sobre la clase media en Cuba," Theo. R. Crevenna, ed., *Materiales para el estudio de la clase media en la América Latina*. Washington, 1950.

Cherne, Leo. "Rum, Sugar, Tourists and Dollars," *Saturday Review* (October 18, 1952).

Cloyd, Joseph. "Our Gayest Neighbor," *American Magazine* (September, 1955).

Cronan, E. David. "Interpreting the Good Neighbor Policy: The Crisis of 1933," *The Hispanic American Historical Review* (November, 1959).

Grobart, Fabio. "Los problemas del desarrollo del partido y la reforma de los estatutos," Partido Socialista Popular, *Los Socialistas y la Realidad Cubana*. Havana, 1946.

Marinello, Juan. "Carta a Antonio Martínez Bello," Martínez Bello, Antonio, *Ideas sociales y económicas de José Martí*. Havana, 1940.

Márquez Sterling, Manuel. "Tejera político," *El Fígaro* (November 15, 1903).

Meeker, Oden. "Cuba Under Batista: More Apathy than Disaffection," *The Reporter* (September 14, 1954).

Ortiz, Fernando. "El deber norteamericano en Cuba," Sociedad Económica de Amigos del País, *Recepción de los Socios de Méritos*. Havana, 1934.

Portell-Vilá, Herminio. "By Way of Prologue," Fernando Ortiz, *Cuban Counterpoint: Tobacco and Sugar*. New York, 1947.

————. "La industria azucarera y su futuro," *Revista Bimestre Cubana*, L (September-October, 1942).

Portuondo, José A. "Cuba, Nación 'Para Si'," *Cuadernos Americanos*, CXIX (November-December, 1961).

Raggi Ageo, Carlos M. "Contribución al estudio de las clases medias en Cuba," Theo R. Crevenna, ed., *Materiales para el estudio de la clase media en la América Latina*. Washington, 1950.

Rama, Carlos M. "América Latina y la primera internacional," *Cuadernos Americanos*, XXIV (January-February, 1965).

Rivero Muñíz, José. "La lectura en las tabaquerías," *Revista de la Biblioteca Nacional* (October-December, 1951).

Roig de Leuchsenring, Emilio. "La lucha cubana contra la Enmienda Platt, la intervención y el imperialismo," *Universidad de la Habana*, XII (June-July, 1937).

Shapiro, Samuel. "Cuba: A Dissenting Report," *The New Republic* (September 12, 1960).

Schulberg, Budd. "Budd Schulberg on Cuba," *Saturday Review* (October 18, 1952).

Thompson, Charles A. "The Cuban Revolution: Fall of Machado," *Foreign Policy Reports*, XI (December 18, 1935).

————. "The Cuban Revolution: Reform and Reaction," *Foreign Policy Reports*, XI (January 1, 1936).

Woodward, Ralph L. "Urban Labor and Communism in Cuba," Caribbean Studies, III (October, 1963).

Index